YORKSHIRE COOKERY

Contents

List of illustrations

Acknowledgment

I should like to thank the following people for their help in providing recipes and information: Mrs Bryant; Kit Calvert; Ella Cansfield; Ian Dewhurst and the staff of Keighley and Colne Libraries; Penny Glanville; Isobelle Gott; Mrs Greenwood; William Holt; Albert Hirst and his firm of Barnsley; Mrs J. Hopper of the Black Swan Hotel, Helmsley; Miss A. Jackson; Roy J. Sabine, Barnsley News Pictures; Mrs M.E. Scott and Mrs N. Young.

Useful assistance has also been provided by the English Tourist Board; Leeds City Reference Library and Leeds University Library, the Blanche Leigh Collection; the Ministry of Agriculture, Fisheries and Food, Hull; the National Market Traders Federation and in particular the market managers of many towns; the Rhubarb Growers Association; the Royal Hotel, Scarborough; T. and R. Theakston Ltd; the White Fish Authority and the Yorkshire Federation of Women's Institutes. I am grateful to the staff of all these organizations but would like to give an especial word of appreciation to the W.I. who have been so helpful and co-operative. Also Cassell Ltd who gave permission to reproduce certain recipes.

For their permission to reproduce the black and white photographs—J. Allan Cash (p.126); Kenneth Scowen (pp.8 and 75); Will F. Taylor (p.65); John Topham (pp.45, 103 and 115); Gerald Wilson (p.56) and York Public Library (p.33). The picture on page 132 is from the publishers' own collection.

To all those friends who have helped me by giving their hospitality and sharing their family recipes I owe a special mention.

Finally and most importantly, thanks to my marvellous family for their support and encouragement—not least in the cheerful way in which they willingly tackled all types of hitherto unknown dishes.

Yorkshire

'If we consider its superior magnitude—it is well entitled to pre-eminence.'
William Marshall of Yorkshire in *Rural Economy of Yorkshire*, 1788

Yorkshire is a county abounding in superlatives, with enough records broken and achievements made to confront the visitors at every turn. Yorkshire cooks prepared the biggest pie ever cooked in England as well as the largest banquet ever held in the country. It seems in keeping that the heaviest Englishman ever recorded, Henry Cooper of Scugdale, also came from Yorkshire; he weighed 29 stone and stood 8 ft 6 in. tall.

Because of its sheer size, variations in traditional dishes tend to occur more in Yorkshire than in other counties. This must be obvious when one considers the contrasts in scenery and physical features, each geographical division resulting in some variation in agriculture.

Conservatism has encouraged the survival of many of Yorkshire's regional dishes. Despite their loss elsewhere they survive as a bastion against mass production in Yorkshire where pride in one's country and a love of 'good, plain cooking' have combined successfully to perpetuate a wealth of traditional recipes.

Yorkshire is too large a county for generalizations. There is no uniformity here, not even in speech—the broad dialect of the North Yorkshire Moors is quite unlike that heard in South Yorkshire or in the villages of the east coast. In a country threatened by mass uniformity it is good to go into an area where individualism still flourishes. Mercifully, the northern spirit is not yet entirely neatened and polished. In some of the more isolated, hilly regions, men still accept honest struggle as a part of life which is necessary if satisfaction in a goal achieved is to be attained. Men here desire to be treated as people, as individuals, as souls; they will continue to take pride in their county's idiosyncracies and differences. Long may the new administrative boundaries be ignored by all those with a feeling for the uniqueness of England and each of her counties.

Yorkshire is the largest of these and contains most requirements for self-sufficiency. On the east coast the ports supply a good proportion of the country's total fish harvest; coal is plentiful and provides heat and energy; millstone grit is here for building, and large expanses of arable and pasture lands produce vegetables and corn in plenty, as well as fodder for the sheep and cattle raised here. These in turn provide food and wool.

Perhaps the inbred knowledge of this abundance has, over centuries, given the Yorkshireman his confidence and liberality, often demonstrated in generously warm hospitality. But while assured enough to boast that he is never afraid to speak his mind, the Yorkshireman can sometimes be guilty of a startling bluntness.

To give a picture of Yorkshire it is best to describe it by the regions into which it naturally falls: the Pennine Dales; the Vale of York; the Cleveland Plain; the North Yorkshire Moors; the Vale of Pickering; the Wolds and the Holderness Plain.

The Pennine Dales have become increasingly popular to tourists and the villages of Swaledale, Wensleydale and Wharfedale become crowded with holidaymakers during the summer months. Equally lovely and with leafy lanes comparatively free of bustling sightseers are the 'secret' dales. More remote, with no sizeable towns to attract the visitors, these are the pockets of tradition. It is possible to find old people making dishes confined largely to the Dales. Havercake or haverbread is sometimes made in the traditional old way but the backstone on which these oatcakes are cooked has given way to the griddle. The word 'haver', from the Norse 'hafri' meaning oats, points to Scandinavian influence which has predominated here since the early invasions. Porridge remains the favourite breakfast dish in Dales farmhouses as it has since the days when little other than oats were grown in the region. As oatmeal was the staple food here, unique features evolved in cottages and farmhouses alike. Special cupboards or arks in which to store oats were built into the walls. One peculiarity of most homes was a bread fleak. This wooden rack was suspended from the ceiling and on it were laid the cooked oatcakes, known in some areas as tharvecakes. They were left to dry on the bread fleak and then eaten with bacon or cheese.

From this area comes, of course, the famous Wensleydale cheese, whose origins lie in the cheese-making methods of the monks in Yorkshire. The method for making cheese from ewes' milk was brought to Yorkshire by the monks of Jervaulx Abbey. During the Reformation the monks, fleeing from persecution, passed the secret on to the families who sheltered them.

It is still possible to buy good cheese in Yorkshire; Blue Wensleydale is particularly fine and the tradition of selling home-made cream cheeses is continued. Curds and curd tarts are other regional specialities which can be bought in markets.

Said by some to typify his county by his frank and honest approach to life is Kit Calvert, well known in the Pennine Dales as the man who encouraged the continuance of the Wensleydale cheesemaking industry. His factory in Hawes was founded upon sheer determination, hard work and a faith in the quality of Wensleydale cheese which persisted despite governmental red tape and regulations.

Hawes is a small straggling town surrounded by wind-freshened fells and remote passes. To approach the sturdy stone-built community from Wharfedale, across the bleak wild moors and mosses where sheep and a curlew might be the only signs of life for miles, is to appreciate to some extent the quality of life experienced within such a town. Close-knit and sharply aware of the vagaries of nature, the slightest suspicion of change in the weather brings a new concern into the conversation in shops and streets. Apparently unperturbed by the cutting wind sweeping along the narrow street, housewives group to gossip about the news since the previous week's market. With any vague threat of snow an immediate concern is expressed for some farmer or shepherd known to be out on the fells. And it seems that everyone in Hawes has relatives involved with the land.

One of the few people still having the skill to make farmhouse Wensleydale cheese is Mrs Scott, a charming elderly woman of Muker in Swaledale who finds it a great source of amusement that she should be one of the last of the old school of Wensleydale cheesemakers while living in a rival dale. Once a farmer's wife, Mrs Scott is now widowed and retired but is still capable of making a Wensleydale cheese which when mature puts any average factory product to shame.

In the eighteenth century Cleveland cheese was the most renowned of Yorkshire cheeses and was described as 'a very good cheese, not inferior to that of Gloucestershire'. Coverbridge, Swaledale and Cotherstone cheeses were local variations of Wensleydale cheese and were all sold at the three-day Yarm Fair each October. During the Fair of 1820, almost seven hundred carts entered the town. Hundreds, perhaps even thousands of cheeses were laid upon clean straw by farmers renting sections of the market place. People from all over the north flocked here to trade and, according to contemporary accounts, the variety and quality of Yorkshire cheeses on sale was unsurpassed.

The good pasture lands of the Dales made it a cattle-raising area, but not generally for beef. Cattle kept solely for beef in the hilly districts were extremely expensive to rear, for the lack of abundant natural vegetation made it necessary to buy fodder which proved prohibitively expensive. Such cattle were not normally kept for home consumption and after being sent to some lowland region for fattening would be sold in cattle markets. Dairy cattle were reared for home milk consumption whenever possible but where increasing industrialization created large markets, the farmers extended their herds. Dairy farming is now concentrated in those parts of Yorkshire having good outlets. The wealthy, expanding markets of Teesside caused the stabilization of dairying on the Cleveland Plain as the markets of Hull did with dairying on the Holderness Plain. Within the Pennine Dales, developing towns to the east provided farmers with the impetus to raise beef cattle which were fattened in the Craven district. Although the Dales were famed for pasture land, producing top quality milk and cheese, the Craven area became notable for the superiority of its beef cattle. Skipton became even more important as a market town and remains the market centre for the Pennine Dales. It is ideally situated for its role and farmers gravitate here from all over the West Riding as well as from the more northern dales. The picturesque main street, dominated by the church at one end and narrow cobbled alleys along the other, is lined by stalls selling everything from 'barley-fed pork' to muffins and oatcakes on market days.

The Vale of York extends north to south through Yorkshire for almost ninety miles and has been described as the heart of the county. It is the richest area agriculturally, with a similarity in cultivation throughout. In general, wheat and barley form seventy-five per cent of the total acreage, and corn is also grown.

In this fertile area 'cash-roots' farming is widespread. Sugar beet, potatoes, cabbage, carrots and Brussels sprouts are cultivated extensively. In the south of this district peas are grown widely to supply the canning and freezing industries. It was recorded in 1688 that the three types of farm in this region were mixed, cattle and corn. These still predominate and on the mixed or 'cash-root' farms vegetables usually form twenty-five per cent of the acreage.

Markets in these vegetable growing areas seem to excel in high quality produce. Crisp, dark spinach from Studley is available in season in Ripon market. Carrots, cauliflower, potatoes, all grown locally, are arranged in appetizing piles on the stalls of Thirsk and Northallerton markets. Leeks, Brussels sprouts, spring cabbage and rhubarb are easily obtainable and in beautiful condition. Mrs Hopper of the Black Swan Hotel in Helmsley is fortunate enough to have her interest in good food aided and encouraged by the quality of vegetables obtainable locally. Although her hotel is just within the hilly Dales area she is able to buy fresh produce from convenient markets on the Vale of York. These are served appetizingly crisp with main course meals which also rely upon local produce for freshness and quality, and upon the expertise of a gourmet to create notable dishes using locally caught game. Mrs Hopper remarked, 'We mostly use grouse caught in the district. In the summer we have grouse, usually for York Race Week in August and our customers enjoy them plain roasted and very rare. We do though serve grouse and quail stuffed with raspberries, butter and spices.'

Any milk production on the Vales of York and Pickering is on a small scale to supply local markets. It has been possible to provide permanent pasture for cattle along the banks of the rivers but in general the Vale of York is not a livestock region. One exception is in the rich farming land around Bedale, one of the best stock fattening areas in England. This prosperous old market town is village-like in atmosphere and never more so than on Tuesdays when the streets are thronged with visitors and farming families come to trade in the market. In 1251 Alan o' Bedale was granted a market charter by King Henry III and to hear some of the stallholders talk with such pride about their market and the length of time their own families have 'stood the market' one might believe them to be direct descendants of those original tradesmen.

The road from Pontefract to Barnsley is a surprising one to strangers expecting industrialization to dominate south Yorkshire. Barnsley has the good fortune to be a thriving industrial town set in an area of attractive villages and rolling, open fields. Although parts of the town have been spoiled in the name of progress, the new market complex is claimed by many Yorkshire people to be the finest in the country. Local delicacies such as black pudding, elder and tripe can be bought as well as gigantic Barnsley chops or delicatessen-type food from many countries of the world.

Also in this area and worth a visit for its market is Dewsbury, a shoddy town and once the only place in the world where auctions of rags were held. Perhaps typical of the Yorkshire spirit at its worst, Dewsbury is vigorously brash and noisy but the genuine friendliness of the town offsets any sinking feeling that might initially overcome the visitor. This interest in the stranger and an eagerness to help is nowhere more apparent than in the small fish market, held twice weekly on Wednesdays and Saturdays. Here the stallholders are free with advice as to the type of fish best suited to one's purpose and are even willing to discuss the best methods of cooking. Sparkling stalls are freshly dressed with parsley and shells to create a setting suitable for the pristine arrays of fish, almost sea-damp in freshness. Shining eyes stare up at the customer from every kind of fish caught from off the Yorkshire coast and beyond. Mother-of-pearl colours gleam from plump mackerel, and enormous snowy steaks of cod, russet tones of smoked herring and haddock and the silver sheen of fresh plaice entice the cook—fish second to none in quality.

Another market which is well worth visiting is that in the city of York itself. To walk round the end section of York market on Saturday mornings is to take a step into the past; to days when markets were the source of fresh food prepared and sold with assurance by country people who took great pride in the high quality of their produce. The part of York market with the greatest charm is that where farmers' wives sit on low benches around open stalls with freshly made parkins, gingerbreads and curd tarts spread out before them; free-range eggs and home-made butter nestle side by side with posies of wild violets and bunches of fresh herbs. Unskinned rabbits, newly killed fowl and jars of golden honey are sold by farmwives from as far afield as Selby and Knaresborough. Vegetables pulled from the garden that morning are displayed to their best advantage. Pots of home-made jams, marmalade and lemon curd stand beside jars holding bunches of pussy-willow gathered from country lanes and bought eagerly by visiting town dwellers. One concession to the twentieth century is the containers. Small plastic bags might hold crisp brandy snaps or snowy-white curds, the latter are sold to anyone wishing to make their own Yorkshire curd tarts. Bags of biscuits known as shortcakes are deceptive. It is easy to equate these with sweet shortbread but in Yorkshire small pieces of pastry are sold as shortcakes to be eaten buttered, with cheese.

The Cleveland Plain is a district of mixed farming on good arable land with corn accounting for half the total yield. In the eighteenth century, Marshall referred to this region as good wheat and bean land producing corn, butter, store cattle and horses. Tuke wrote in 1794: 'Wheat is the staple produce of Cleveland. No other district in The Riding, or perhaps in the North of England, produces as much in proportion to its size, or of as good a quality.'

Also in the north-east are the North Yorkshire Moors. The land here is chiefly of a poor acid nature, marshy in parts. Where it is well drained a more reasonable level of agriculture has been possible and especially in those valleys crossing the moorland. Until the mid-eighteenth century, rye was the chief crop and rye bread a staple food. Towards the end of the century wheat was grown more extensively, as happened in Cleveland and gradually wheaten bread replaced the traditional rye bread of this moorland region.

During the eighteenth century probably twenty to thirty thousand sheep in all were kept on moorland farms. Sheep farming has usually been the only type possible on the moors and has always been carried out at subsistence level. The moorland areas of the industrial West Riding, the North Yorkshire Moors and the Pennine Dales are the parts of the county now synonymous with sheep. These are the areas where mutton can be bought in small butchers' shops and regional delicacies such as hot mutton pies and spiced mutton are occasionally obtainable in restaurants.

Grouse and rabbits are caught on the moorlands of Yorkshire and on the Wolds, although shooting is now strictly regulated. In the past, rabbits were a valuable source of meat and warrens were often contained within walls built from sods and fenced on top. These sometimes enclosed two thousand acres and it has been estimated that in the early nineteenth century there were twenty warrens enclosing ten thousand acres. Turnips and grass were sown especially to feed the rabbits which would eventually be sold in the developing industrial towns of the West Riding or in the large markets of York and Hull.

One highly localized crop grown in Yorkshire is rhubarb, which has flourished around Leeds since the Industrial Revolution. It became centralized in Leeds because of climatic and soil conditions as well as having good communications and marketing outlets. There are now sixty to seventy rhubarb growers concentrated in the Leeds–Dewsbury–Wakefield district. Plants are grown for two years before being put into unlit sheds for forcing. Conditions here are highly specialized, the sheds being kept warm, moist and dark at all times. Even during picking only candles or lanterns are used to keep the darkness as intense as possible.

Locally grown rhubarb is eagerly looked for in springtime in the towns of the West Riding. It is thought to be far superior to any other fruit obtainable in the season and rhubarb pies and puddings dominate the tea-tables of housewives proud of their home-baking.

A very popular event in rhubarb-growing areas last century was 'T'Rhubarb Charity'. This was organized annually by chapel congregations and everyone around seemed to participate. The idea was apparently to enjoy some entertainment, usually 'a good sing' to the music of a local band, share an abundant tea of home-made foods, always including rhubarb pies or dishes of stewed rhubarb, then to contribute to the collection held in aid of local charities.

Another crop concentrated in the West Riding was liquorice, introduced by monks during the thirteenth century for medicinal purposes and later grown as a sweetmeat. Some thirteen years ago the only liquorice growers remaining in Pontefract went out of business. Mr Booth and Mr Carter were last of a long line of liquorice farmers. Now the famous Pontefract Cakes are manufactured from imported liquorice. The round, flat sweets are extremely popular and have contributed greatly to the town's prosperity. Although the blue-flowered liquorice plant is no longer grown on a large scale, untreated liquorice root is still to children from local chemists' shops.

The Vale of Pickering was once noted for its prosperous fruit farms but is now predominately arable with some dairying. It provides a high proportion of the country's barley harvest. The one soft fruit grown here in any quantity is the gooseberry, a fruit which causes even phlegmatic Yorkshiremen to grow passionate during annual contests to determine the largest fruit.

At one time there was a small although thriving pork industry centred upon Pickering, a dignified little town built round an old market square surrounded by mellow limestone buildings. Barrels of salt pork were supplied to whaling ships at Whitby and cured hams were sent to hotels in London and Edinburgh. This was at the end of the nineteenth century and compared to present-day mammoth enterprises was just a cottage industry.

Two features of interest in the Pickering area for the gourmet are the watercress beds and the trout farm. The watercress beds utilize water from the River Costa, flowing to the south of the town. The trout farm at Newbridge is the largest in the country selling a ton of fish each week. Even so, the owner Mike O'Donnell says he is unable to produce enough smoked trout to satisfy the demand. The only way in which he could do this would be by expanding even more and by using rapid, highly commercialized methods. This he prefers not to do, believing that only by using traditional methods and oak sawdust can a delicately flavoured smoked trout be produced. He explains: 'We only do a mild smoke, our customers prefer to get the taste of trout; otherwise they may as well eat kipper. Oak is renowed for the best flavours and we in Yorkshire are lucky in having good supplies.'

Interestingly, the sawdust used in smoking the fish comes from the workshops of 'Mousey' Thompson at Kilburn. This family of wood-craftsmen lovingly carve a tiny mouse on each piece of work.

The rolling hills of the Wolds can be compared with the Downlands of southern England, with billowing fields showing white chalk flecks against the dark ploughed earth. The boundary hedges too have more in common with the Downs than with other parts of Yorkshire. In the exposed moorlands, drystone walls have been the only feasible means of enclosing fields for few trees survive the rigours of moorland winters. Stone or chalk cottages surround village greens in these sparsely populated Wolds, a pond or well sometimes adding an even more picturesque touch to the scene. The villagers one meets are, however, totally northern in outlook. No picture-postcard villages these but communities bonded by struggle and adversity. Shallow soil and poor climatic conditions caused by the altitude of the region have made it difficult to eke out a living from the land unless vast acreages are involved, and low average yields have caused the closure of many farms.

The chalky Wolds were predominately sheep-rearing regions, until the extension of corn cultivation in the eighteenth century. Here wheat and barley predominate but corn is now being developed as a major crop.

The most important influence on the development of sheep-rearing in Yorkshire were the monasteries. Few parts of England were settled by monasteries on such a large scale and Cistercians came here because much of the land was regarded as 'waste'. Expert research has proved that the concentration of monastic houses was greatest where wasteland could be reclaimed. As land was settled and farmed, sheep flocks flourished under the guidance of the Cistercians, described as the world's most skilful sheep farmers. Benedictine monks contributed their own special knowledge and there grew up a highly prosperous wool trade in Yorkshire. Continental merchants clamoured for high quality wool and became regular traders at the wool fairs of Beverley and York. Fountains Abbey owned almost a third of the county of Yorkshire by the end of the thirteenth century. Whitby Abbey kept four thousand sheep during the early part of the following century and Rievaulx is estimated to have owned a flock of twelve thousand sheep during the same period. With the decline in the wool trade and the dissolution of the monasteries, the size of flocks decreased.

The strong influence of the monastic settlements in Yorkshire can still be felt in the rural areas where there was a strong tradition of healing. Monks were respected not only for their religious work but for the healing powers they exercised in times of sickness and plague. Their gardens contained plants grown for medicinal as well as for culinary purposes. Expanses of some of these plants can be found in the locality of ruined religious houses and are used by elderly people who have faith in their curative properties. Large patches of valerian and garlic in the woods near Bolton Abbey are picked by local people and made into medicines. Bog myrtle was grown by monks for making Gale Beer and the sweet herb is still gathered for this purpose.

Two of the most typical Wolds towns are Pocklington and Market Weighton. The latter is a plain, pleasant country market town. Unpretentious and friendly, the people have an intense pride in their little town and are quick to point out its attractions. Drifting among the farmers in local hostelries, one is instantly made aware of the agricultural leanings of the region; talk is almost entirely of corn—quality, quantity and prices hoped for, but never of prices attained.

Within easy reach of Pocklington, the village of Millington has an attractive Wolds setting and has an inn where home-made meat pie with traditional mushy peas is served at weekends. The landlord will also pull a pint of Theakston's Old Peculiar for the discerning visitor. This beer, one of the strongest in the country, is brewed in Masham, near Ripon. Old Peculiar is a barley wine type of beer brewed to a secret, century-old recipe and is available on draught at a number of Yorkshire public houses. It was named after a local ecclesiastical court which dealt with cases arising from the vicar's rights in this 'Peculiar' parish. Among other unique powers the vicar had the right to license midwives and apothecaries.

Traditionally brewed ale comes also from Timothy Taylor and Co. Ltd of

Keighley. Their Draught Landlord is a strong, nutty beer served at an ancient hostelry in Chisley, near Hebden Bridge. Described by one local expert as 'toothsome', the ale is cheerfully and expertly served by the landlord who also cooks and serves simple, well-prepared meals to order. He prides himself on the freshness of his food, buying daily from local tradesmen and making soup according to whatever is available. Specialities are mushroom and mixed vegetable. Some traditional specialities are black puddings and fish and chips.

Barley produced in the Vale of Pickering and in the Wolds at one time accounted for a sizeable proportion of that used in Yorkshire's breweries. With the enormous increase in demand since the Second World War, much of the barley has had to be imported.

The Holderness Plain was described in the eighteenth century as fenland but later that century and during the next, extensive drainage was undertaken. Rich and fertile farmland resulted and in the nineteenth century the chief crops were corn and potatoes with peas and beans becoming traditional to the district. These provided the basis for substantial local dishes such as pease pudding and vegetable rolls.

Vegetables produced on the Holderness Plain are not only marketed in the eastern part of the county but in the industrial towns of the West Riding. Shops in Halifax, Huddersfield and Dewsbury rely upon growers on the Plain for vegetables. William Holt of Hebden Bridge explained: 'Our main suppliers are in the Hull area. We get very few vegetables grown commercially around here, the soil is too poor and the weather too wet.' Fresh milk and broiler fowl are also produced commercially on the plain.

Pig-raising in Yorkshire has centered in Holderness, principally because of the densely populated region around Kingston upon Hull which provides an enormous market for farm products. Pigs are still kept, chiefly on a small scale, all over Yorkshire.

Finally, we have the ports and their neighbouring areas. Yorkshire is well endowed with good fishmongers' shops and market stalls, perhaps not surprising when one considers that the total catch of fish landed at Hull in 1974 weighed 2,822,588 cwt making it one of the most important fishing ports in the country. The second largest port in Yorkshire is Scarborough with a catch of 85,001 cwt in 1974. Of this 1,575 cwt was in crabs and 298 cwt in lobsters and 38 cwt in queens. Shellfish landed in Hull weighed only 5 cwt, these being squids.

The types of fish landed in the other Yorkshire ports differ greatly. In all, cod amounted to the greatest total weight of fish landed in 1974 and 1975 with haddock second in Redcar and Staithes but whiting weighed in as the second heaviest catch at Bridlington, Scarborough and Whitby.

All these ports of Yorkshire are worth a visit, not only for themselves, but for the culinary treats that can be found.

Whitby is a picturesque resort of some historical interest and has a particular fascination for visitors who can watch the sun both rise and set over the sea on this part of the coast. Travelling north from Whitby one passes along a steep road before reaching the quaint fishing village of Staithes. An interesting hour on out-of-season evenings can be spent in the Cod and Lobster Inn, for here local fishermen congregate to mull over the day's fishing, comparing catches with those of the same months of other years.

If, instead of going north to Staithes, one follows the A171 road to Guisborough across the Cleveland Hills, one realizes just how desolate the region must have been several centuries ago when it was virtually uninhabited. Even now it is rare to see a person outside a moving vehicle in the whole twenty miles. The solitude is almost tangible and greatly valued by the lover of open spaces and quiet when one walks half a mile away from the road almost anywhere along its length. It is probably at its best early in the year, or in the autumn when thickly smudged with the royal purple tones of the heather.

Leaving Whitby by the A169 one travels across the long expanses of open moorland towards the hamlet of Saltersgate. Between Sleights and Saltergate one passes, or stops at if interested in good food, an inn where a Whitby lobster is most succulently prepared in cocktail form.

Turning right here along the narrow road one is always surprised to see the little wooded valley of Egton Bridge after the lonely, deserted stretches of moorland. This quaint village is the scene of much activity on one day of the year when the 'Berry Show' is held. This was started early last century to encourage the growing of gooseberries in the area. Sizes attained are phenomenal—it seems unbelievable that these shiny, swollen fruits could really be gooseberries. Each one is weighed individually and a Yorkshireman invariably claims the championships. In 1978 however, to local chagrin, the winning monster was grown by a Cheshire man.

Back on the main road and on to Saltersgate which gained its name in days when it was a stopping place on a salt route from the sea. Here one can always be sure of seeing at the Wagon and Horses Inn a turf fire glowing, which is said to have burned continuously for over a hundred years. From here the road sweeps upwards then gradually drops down to Pickering (see page 16).

Yorkshire's largest port, Hull, is a city of contrasts of old and new; shopping centres compete with the lure of the docks for the attention of the visitor. Anyone with the smallest amount of imagination is mentally transported to all parts of the world when reading the names and home ports of ships standing in the port of Hull.

One of the loveliest of Yorkshire's cities is Beverley, only about eight miles out of Hull. This beautiful, ancient town has the advantage of two market places. One is the 'Saturday Market' with an eighteenth-century market cross, the other is the 'Wednesday Market'. The market is now only held on Saturdays but is a perfect, country-type market with just enough bustle and noise to create interest.

Almost directly north of Hull is the much smaller but equally interesting Bridlington. You can reach it from Hull by travelling across the low-lying coastal plain. The lively markets of Bridlington can be enjoyed by locals twice weekly and are naturally plentifully stocked with the dairy produce and fresh vegetables produced on the land between Bridlington and Hull. Stallholders here are infected with that cheerful breeziness which seems to characterize all the coastal area from Filey to Easington. This is perhaps an instance of the climate affecting the character, for certainly this district appears accustomed to an ever-present wind.

One town along this stretch of coast which has become less important as a port since medieval days is Hornsea, which is now a thriving seaside resort. It also possesses Yorkshire's largest lake, Hornsea Mere, which was once greatly valued for its fish and in monastic days the right to fish here was claimed by two houses. Tradition has it that the argument became so fierce between monks of Meaux Abbey, near Beverley and St Mary's Abbey, York that blows were struck and a fight developed beside the mere. York proved the stronger and might was held to be right but the monks of Meaux were allowed to fish freely along the southern bank of the lake.

Special Yorkshire Traditions

Breakfast   Egg and bacon was the breakfast enjoyed by every yeoman farmer or statesman of the Dales. Otherwise, a thick slice of cold, home-cured bacon or ham would be enjoyed with oatcakes or home-made bread. This, washed down with copious amounts of strong tea, is still the breakfast eaten by many farmers.

High Teas   The great Yorkshire tradition for high teas still survives in rural communities and elsewhere at weekends, when families visit on Sundays to share in the meal which has become symbolic of good home cooking.

It is as unthinkable to serve high tea in 'dribs and drabs' as it would be to serve packeted Yorkshire pudding. Everything is placed upon the table at the start of the meal and as much as possible is home-made, from the bread to the pickles.

Between five and six o'clock is still the accepted time for high tea, fitting in well with workers arriving home, children being back from school. On Sundays, it is also the most convenient time for all the family and as well it enables the washing-up to be done before evening services at chapel or church. It was in the nineteenth century that high tea became a fashionable meal in London and other cities. Mrs Beeton wrote: 'At the usual High Tea there are probably to be found one or two small hot dishes, cold chickens, or game, tongue or ham, salad, cakes of various kinds, sometimes cold fruit tarts with cream or custard and fresh fruits.'

Although these generous and abundant spreads are no longer fashionable, they are a normal occurrence in Yorkshire, land of the trencherman. A Barnsley butcher's wife told me that one essential part of the high tea 'spread' in her family was her spice loaf. She described her cake as 'a nice homely loaf with middlin' of fruit in and a little pinch of spice in. They just touch the palate.'

Earlier this century a Sunday high tea would often have tinned salmon as the *pièce de résistance* but home-made pies of all kinds were much more popular with the men. Yorkshire high teas did, however, tend to be remarkable in the emphasis laid upon boiled ham. Boiled ham became a symbol of respectability towards the end of the nineteenth century when it was everyone's hope to be 'buried with boiled ham'. A respectable funeral was synonymous with a boiled ham tea, so much so that boiled ham is still sometimes referred to by older people as 'slow-walking bread'.

The great distinction between a typical high tea and a funeral tea was that in some families it was considered 'fast' or 'flighty' to serve anything sweet at a funeral tea. Boiled ham, pickles and home-made bread or tea-cakes were respectable. Spice-cake, curd tarts, tipsy cake and parkin were not. One type of biscuit which was acceptable to all was the funeral biscuit. Either baked at home or ordered from a confectioner who advertised the fact that he specialized in 'funeral bread and biscuits', they were given to the mourners to take home. Sometimes the white paper in which they were wrapped was sealed with black sealing wax. Several old people have described to me how when they were children they looked forward to receiving the small package from parents who had attended a funeral. Many of them describe the biscuits or biskeys as being like a plain Yorkshire tea-cake. Others remember that they were slightly sweetened, contained caraway seeds and were called 'funeral cakes'. Some families owned engraved wooden stamps which were only used to impress patterns on funeral biscuits. These were handed down through generations and were greatly prized. Early in the nineteenth century a typical funeral tea might comprise oatcakes and cheese or ham with white bread if the family were prosperous. Perhaps the origin of the use of boiled ham as a traditional part of Yorkshire funeral or high teas lies in the fact that ham was available to anyone having land on which to keep a pig. Anyone without pig-keeping facilities was poor indeed during the industrialized nineteenth century.

The food was appreciated by mourners who had travelled long distances and each would later take home some funeral bread to eat with his family in remembrance of the dead person. In the Keighley area funeral teas were known as Arvills; in other parts of Yorkshire funeral bread was called Arvill bread. The derivation is Nordic, from the word 'Arveol' which was a feast held in honour of a dead chief and at which the succession was declared. 'Arvel' was sometimes used to mean the ale distributed at a funeral tea, just as 'Bridal' was the ale given out at weddings.

It is now rare for funeral teas to be as rigidly traditional as they were but Isobelle Gott of Lothersdale caters for families wishing to follow the customary practice. She is dedicated to preserving all that is good in Yorkshire food and presents a traditional funeral ham tea with all the customary accompaniments. She also makes brawn, pickles ox-tongues and bakes a comprehensive range of what she herself describes as 'old-fashioned standbyes'. Her country teas are a delight, and even the butter is home-made, spread generously upon crusty, newly baked bread. Mrs Gott explained:

> To lose a young member of a family in a country village was accepted with quiet grief by the whole village and it was not an unusual occurence, but the passing of a veteran brought relations and friends from a wide area in dog carts, etc. and many on foot. It was expected there would be a tea afterwards, usually held in the chapel room. I still offer this service and most of my receipts have been handed down from Granny Brown to Grandma Clarke to me. One of my most popular cakes is Grandma Clarke's Scones [page 122] but Auntie Belle's Parkin [page 112] is very well liked. One of our favourites at home is my own Seed Cake [page 114]. Good, home-made food is always preferred by my family and by the people I cater for in the village. They expect and I prefer to make the wholesome but attractive Yorkshire dishes.

Early this century, cyclists and walkers began to travel extensively through Yorkshire at weekends. They sought the generous peace of the countryside and almost all of those recollecting these times recall the high teas served in farmhouses by farmwives eager to satisfy the appetites of 'whey-faced townies' with wholesome country food. Boiled ham or ham and eggs were inevitable and few young men could resist the appetizing plates of food pressed generously upon them with such admonishments as 'Now eat oop. I know young lads 'as a bottomless drop.'

Christmas   In the past, food and tradition were closely interwoven. Most of the Church's festivals were celebrated with feasting at which a traditional dish was served and none more lustily than at Christmas-time.

Many of the Christmas traditions of the north are attributed to Nordic influences. Boar's flesh was a legendary food in Valhalla, the place in Norse mythology where the souls of slain heroes feasted. The Nordic festival of 'Yule' was absorbed into Christian festivities and until recently the Yule Log or Yule Clog was an important feature of Yorkshire Christmas tradition.

Washington Irving described the bearing in of the boar's head at one Christmas dinner he attended in Yorkshire when the 'table was literally loaded with good cheer, and presented an epitome of country abundance, in this season of overflowing larders. A distinguished post was alloted to "ancient sirloin," as mine host termed it; being, as he added, "the Standard of old English hospitality, and a joint of goodly presence, and full of expectations." ' An amusing situation arose when Irving admired a pie strikingly dressed with peacock's feathers, but which his host honestly admitted to be pheasant pie. So many of his peacocks had died during the season that he could not bring himself to have another one killed. Also on the table was a turkey given a very summary mention, perhaps not being one of the traditional dishes in which Washington Irving was so interested.

In medieval days a prosperous Yorkshire family might have enjoyed goose, boar's head, frumety and a roasted baron of beef for their Christmas feast but it was to be many years before turkey featured in the festive meal. Conservative as all country people, Yorkshire families in rural districts still tend to prefer the traditional beef and ham at Christmas-time.

Note

Many of the recipes in this book have been included primarily for their historical interest and have been adapted as far as possible to take into account our modern ingredients and cooking processes. Both metric and imperial quantities are given—the metric quantities are not exact conversions, but are adjusted to give equally successful results. It is important, therefore, to follow either all-metric or all-imperial measurements and not to mix the two.

Meat

Meat

Mutton was the meat most frequently used in Yorkshire until Victorian days when beef became more favoured; now mutton is difficult to obtain except in some small towns where butchers supply it for those older customers appreciating its flavour.

Until Elizabethan days it was rare for beef to appear on the table at all in most homes. The nobility, merchants and farmers would be able to buy fresh meat in summer or to raise their own beasts, then through the winter the meat would be eaten salted. The peasantry usually ate fish or home-produced salt pork or bacon. Lack of winter fodder caused them to kill their pigs around October and November, when they had a little fresh meat (usually offal) before the rest was salted. With the coming of enclosures, cottagers were unable to turn their pigs on to open land so fatty pork and bacon were denied them. By this time, sheep farming had become so well established in Yorkshire that mutton was available to all who could afford it.

The wealth of the farmer depended upon his animals and land so that he was unwilling to sacrifice young stock to the table. Consequently, neither lamb nor veal were ever popular in Yorkshire, calves especially only being killed when diseased so that veal was always suspect.

Pork

In his *The Food of London* (1856), George Dodd wrote 'What species of animal will most economically convert vegetable produce into meat fitted for the butcher?—The cottager estimates very highly the omnivorous qualities of his pig, manifested as they are by the disappearance of all sorts of waste and offal, thus rendering the purchase of food scarcely necessary.'

William Cobbett had written of pig-killing in his book *Cottage Economy* in 1824; '. . . here in the mere offal, in the mere garbage, there is food, and delicate food, too, for a large family for a week, and hogs' puddings for the children, and some for the neighbours' children who come to play with them.'

Nothing at all was wasted from the killing of a pig and the day after the animal was cut up, it was customary to carry pieces of meat to friends who would reciprocate when their pig was killed.

The carefully butchered carcase was divided into joints intended for bacon or hams and pieces to be eaten as pork. York hams have been famed for their flavour for centuries, the first ones having been supposedly smoked in oak sawdust gathered during work on the interior of York Minster.

When pork was roasted the skin was scored and spread with lard and the joint cooked on a rack inside a tin so that the skin would not become toughened by the fat but would cook to a rich golden crispness. This method was only employed in large households while most families contented themselves with boiled meat. Joints of pork were usually cooked in large pots over the fire with a mixture of vegetables, herbs, seasoning and a spoonful of treacle. Small suetcrust dumplings might be dropped in for the last minutes of cooking and when these had risen fluffily, the hearty meal would be served. It has been customary to serve apples with pork since the days when pigs were able to root around in woods and orchards for their food, eating windfall apples with relish as part of their inadequate diet.

The fatty meat obtained from pigs in the past was greatly relished by cottagers who preferred the richness of fat meat or bacon. All surplus fat was rendered down for re-use. After the butchering the flead was put into a container on the fire or stove to be melted down into lard. The pig's head was usually made into brawn but sometimes the nose and cheeks were cooked as separate delicacies. Tripe was eaten in the manner of cow's tripe—either eaten cold after cleaning and boiling or cooked with onions in white sauce. The trotters were a prized tea-time treat, usually eaten cold with plenty of salt and vinegar dashed on but sometimes fried or cooked like tripe. Even the bits left from the flead after all the lard had been extracted were fried, sprinkled with salt and vinegar and relished as 'scratchings', eaten alone or with baked potatoes.

The first parts to be eaten after pig-killing were the soft meats. Liver was either fried with bacon or stewed with onions, carrots, turnips and herbs. The chitterlings were washed thoroughly under running water, often a convenient stream, then blanched and eaten in any of the ways tripe might be served. Kidneys were usually added to the stew or suet pudding made with liver. Any small pieces of meat would be made into brawn faggots or pork cheese, or be used for pork pies.

Before all else though, the blood was kept and made into the north-country delicacy, black pudding. Sharing a talent with those great gourmets, the French, northerners have unqualified success in making these puddings, and a Barnsley firm, in business since 1897 and still using the same recipe, has won several awards at the annual competition for blood puddings in France. When England was invited to compete in 1969, Albert Hirst won a gold medal in his first year of entry from among eight hundred competitors, representing eight countries. This 'King of Black Puddings' uses seventy-five per cent meat in his puddings, a lot of blood, fat, onion and sage and other seasonings. Perhaps his 'secret seasoning' is pennyroyal, for one woman in the Pennine Dales deplored the fact to me that pennyroyal is rarely used in black puddings now.

The Yorkshiremen's love of a 'gradely' black pudding is apparent in the number of markets still serving warm puddings with mustard on certain days of the week, especially Saturdays. Some of them also sell plates of cut-up tripe, various types being mixed together to give the customer a good selection—for instance, honeycomb, thick-seam and black tripe. Honeycomb is the favourite for cooking although many like it cold because of the way the 'oiles [holes] 'old the vinegar'.

Lamb and Mutton

Another Barnsley speciality is the Barnsley Chop, which is thought to have originated at the King's Head Hotel, Market Hill, Barnsley, in 1849. Farmers coming into the town for the market regularly visited the King's Head for a meal which usually consisted of an enormous chop. On the visit of the Prince of Wales to Barnsley in 1933, the Barnsley Chop was served for lunch. Seventy-two chops were used for the meal, each weighing 1 lb 6 oz, and were taken from year-old Southdown sheep, each sheep giving two chops.

A traditional Yorkshire seasoning to use with mutton or lamb was the wild thyme or wild mint found growing abundantly in sheep grazing areas. Barberries or rowan-berries were made into jellies to serve with the meat, giving tangy contrast to the sweetness of the mutton. Sometimes chopped herbs were rubbed over mutton before it was smeared with dripping, floured and roasted in a hot oven. Some farmer's wives basted mutton frequently during the cooking, reducing the oven temperature after the meat had been sealed and sprinkling the joint with flour between bastings. They believed that the crusty layer formed over the meat helped to retain the juices. Breast of mutton was also floured, sprinkled with pepper and then fried before being put into an oven dish with fried onions, a bay leaf and peas. Stock was added, not quite enough to cover the meat, then the dish was lidded and cooked slowly.

Fat from the sheep's kidney was often used to make suetcrust pastry for a mutton pudding. The kidney was chopped up and put into a pastry-lined basin with mutton, onions and sweet herbs such as wild thyme, mint or rosemary with perhaps a few barberries. A good stock was poured in, pastry crust was added, then the dish was covered securely and steamed for three hours.

Mutton fat was prized as much as goose-grease on farms, not only for cooking but to use in making ointments or to rub onto boots to make them waterproof. Fat was clarified, often with the addition of lemon juice to remove the strong flavour, then used in baking.

On the whole, slow-cooking dishes were preferred since these resulted in less shrinkage. Yorkshire family recipe books contain an abundance of pies and puddings, stews and hot-pots. Roasting was primarily confined to wealthy homes.

Beef

Beef cattle have not been raised in sufficiently large numbers in Yorkshire for a great tradition in beef cooking to have developed. Yorkshire pudding, perhaps the most famous of the county's dishes, was traditionally served with gravy before the beef course. Rabbit was popular among the working classes of industrial towns, ham or bacon in rural areas, and mutton or lamb was highly regarded everywhere.

During late Victorian days Sunday dinner became the exception to this rule, for many families endeavoured to make this the main meal of the week, usually with roast beef and Yorkshire pudding. Here again, the Yorkshireman cannot be categorized, for all families have individual preferences. Many chose to have baked ham or roast rabbit for Sunday dinner. Although not always to be relied upon, there was usually a supplier of wild rabbits in the neighbourhood of rural localities and it has been suggested that a plate of light, crisp and fluffy Yorkshire pudding served piping hot with wild rabbit gravy and roasted rabbit to follow could not be bettered.

Roast beef was and is always preferred streaked with fat for moistness and served with horse-radish sauce. The sirloin, cooked with the bone, is the most favoured joint and often in Yorkshire it is sprinkled with mustard before cooking to 'bring out the flavour'.

As with pork and mutton, beef was usually served in a pot-cooked form, boiled or braised, pot-roasted or stewed. Another favourite method was to serve meat spiced, either hot, or pressed after cooking and served cold. See pages 31, 32 and 35 for recipes.

Yorkshire people really enjoyed dumplings with their boiled beef but oats were used in a similar way. Gravy from the partially cooked beef in the pot was added to well-seasoned oatmeal to make a firm dough. This was put into a greased cloth, loosely wrapped and tied, then put into the pot to cook with the beef—a hearty and typically Yorkshire combination.

Northerners are renowed for their love of robust dishes, probably a tradition from times when substantial meals had to provide packing and warmth for long days spent working in terrible conditions. Pie shops sprang up in every town at the end of the nineteenth century and did a roaring trade until well after the Second World War. Robert's shop in Bradford was a particular favourite of the people of that city. One old man has told me how he was 'treated' to a steaming hot dish of pie and peas there occasionally by his father. At a stall in Bradford market the same kind of pie could be bought, as could 'trunnel' pie with peas. Trunnel pie was a hot pie filled with tripe pieces.

BEEF

Wakefield Steak

a thick piece of steak approx.
   175g (6 oz)
1 tablespoon Worcester sauce
1 teaspoon dry mustard
1 teaspoon salt
1 teaspoon sugar
½ teaspoon pepper

Make cuts all over the steak and place in a dish. Mix all the other ingredients well and pour over the meat. Leave for 2 or 3 hours, then drain and grill. Melt a knob of butter, add the marinade, and when hot pour over the steak to serve.

serves 1.

Yorkshire Hare

675g (1½lb) beef
2 sticks celery
100g (4 oz) mushrooms
2 carrots
½ small turnip
1 onion
dripping
seasoned flour
4 or 5 cloves
½ teaspoon ground nutmeg
2 tablespoons red wine

This recipe came to me from Huddersfield and was recommended for making any tough beef taste as good as hare.

Cut the beef into strips and roll in seasoned flour and ground nutmeg. Melt some good dripping in a frying pan and fry the beef until browned all over; place in an oven dish with the chopped celery, mushrooms, carrots, and turnip. Peel an onion and stick with the cloves, then put into the dish with very little liquid – perhaps two tablespoons each of water and red wine. Cover tightly and cook for approximately 2½ hours or until tender at 160°C (325°F), Gas Mark 3.

serves 4.

Beef or Mutton Hash

450g (1lb) sliced, cooked beef
   or mutton
beef bones
1 small carrot
1 small onion
½ small turnip
1 scant tablespoon flour
½ teacup mushroom ketchup
½ teaspoon Yorkshire relish
a bunch of mixed herbs, *or*
   some parsley, thyme and a
   bay leaf
seasoning

This recipe came from Bradford and is a tasty method of using leftover meat. Similar recipes were common earlier this century when families bought huge joints for Sunday dinner and then were left with large quantities of cold meat to use as imaginatively as possible.

Prepare all the vegetables. Using 575 ml (1 pint) of water make a stock with the bones, herbs and vegetables, omitting the onion. Cook this stock for 1½ hours, then strain.

Fry the onion in melted fat until brown and gradually stir in the flour, then the ketchup and relish. Season and add the stock slowly, stirring continuously. Allow to cook for a minute before adding the meat slices and heating thoroughly.

For a recipe to make your own Yorkshire relish, see page 38.

serves 4.

Steak and Tripe Hot Pot

225g (½ lb) rump steak
450g (1 lb.) tripe
2 carrots
1 large onion
1 stick of celery
dripping

Cut up the beef and tripe and chop all the vegetables into small pieces. Melt the dripping and when hot fry the cut-up beef until brown on all sides. Remove the beef, pour off any surplus fat and fry the prepared vegetables. Add the beef and pieces of tripe. Season well. Cover tightly, and cook slowly for 1½ hours without adding any liquid.

serves 2-3.

Beverley Spiced Beef

675g (1½ lb) piece of beef
    skirting
1 carrot (optional)
1 onion (optional)
stock
ground cloves
salt
black pepper

Rub the beef well with salt. Leave overnight, then drain and wipe with a clean cloth. Mix together the ground cloves and black pepper and rub into the meat. Roll up tightly, tie securely, and put into a pan with water or stock to cover. A chopped carrot and an onion can be added. Bring to the boil, then cover and simmer until tender — at least 2 hours. Remove the beef and leave under a weighted board until the next day. Serve sliced with salad, or with savoury baked potatoes and freshly made pickled onions, which are highly popular in Yorkshire.

The strained liquid makes an excellent base for soup.

serves 4.

Beef and Cowheel Pie

675g (1½ lb) lean steak
flour
salt and pepper
dripping
½ cowheel
1 onion
shortcrust pastry

This recipe was given to me by a family coming from the Sheffield area and is taken from a manuscript cookery book dated 1878.

'Cut a pound and a half of lean steak into neat pieces and dip each one into flour which has been well seasoned with salt and pepper. Melt some good dripping in your pan and fry the steak until it is brown. Wash half a cowheel in salted water, cut up and put in a dish with your steak. Chop an onion and put this in with enough water to cover, then put on your lid and cook until all the meats are tender. This will take three hours. Cover with a good short crust and cook till nicely browned.'

serves 4.

With this method the bones are retained and if preferred they can be removed from the cowheel before the pastry lid is put on the pie. The writer suggested that black puddings made a very good dish to serve with steak and cowheel pie. The black puddings should be skinned and mashed with a fork and a cup of milk should be added to a pound of black puddings. These are to be well heated in the oven.

Halifax High Tea Beef

1¾kg (4lb) piece of salted
   brisket of beef
225g (½ lb) bacon pieces
2 carrots
1 onion
a bunch of savoury herbs
a good pinch each of ground
   allspice, cloves and mace
seasoning.
stock

Put all the ingredients into an oven dish and cover with water or stock. Cover tightly and bake in a warm oven, 160°C (325°F), Gas Mark 3, until tender—approximately 4 hours. Cool in the liquid, then place the meat on a dish or in a basin and weight heavily. Leave overnight to press, then turn out and serve cold.

serves 6.

Martinmas Beef (1760)

'Take ribs of beef, cut off the thin fat part of the ribs, then salt it well with saltpetre and common salt, and after that is very rubbed in, let the beef lie 10 days. Then drain it well and dredge all over with flour and hang it up 2 or 3 days in a dry place, but not too near a fire, then take it down and light a very little fire in a stove or chimney and throw a few juniper berries into the fire, a few at a time not to make too great a smoke, or some sawdust and hang your beef so that the smoke may come to it. Do this three or four times an hour at a time and hang it in a dry place for use. It will be fit to eat in about four months.'

Shepherd's Pie

450g (1 lb) lean minced beef
1kg (2lb) potatoes
1 large onion
425ml (¾ pint) beef stock
100g (4 oz) butter
150ml (¼ pint) milk
1 round dessertspoon cornflour
beef dripping *or* vegetable oil
tomato purée
seasoning

Melt the dripping or oil and in it cook the sliced onion until golden. Add the beef and stir until brown, then add most of the stock, season and cover. Cook for ½ hour, then add the tomato purée and the cornflour mixed with the remaining stock. Stir well and simmer for 5 minutes. Cook the potatoes and mash them, then melt the butter and pour into the mashed potatoes. Warm the milk, then add and mix with a fork to lighten.

   Put the cooked beef into an oven dish, cover with the potato and bake for 45-60 minutes at 180°C (350°F), Gas Mark 4. If the top is not browned, place the dish under a hot grill for a few minutes.

serves 4.

Steak and Kidney Pie

The filling:

1kg (2 lbs) rump steak
450g (1 lb) kidney
175g (6 oz) mushrooms
1 onion
stock
butter
herbs as liked
flour

suetcrust pastry:
450g (1 lb) flour
175g (6 oz) chopped suet
1 rounded teaspoon baking
    powder
salt and pepper
water

Thoroughly mix all the ingredients for the pastry and stir in just enough cold water to give a firm consistency. Butter a large basin and line this with the pastry, reserving some for a lid.

Cut the meat into neat pieces, trimming off any kidney fat, and roll in well-seasoned flour. Peel and slice the onion finely, then melt the butter and cook the onion in it until soft and golden. Remove from the pan and replace with the meat, adding more butter if necessary, and cook the meat until brown on all sides. Mix together the onion, chopped mushrooms and meat. Add chopped herbs—parsley, tarragon and thyme are good—but use them sparingly, since the chief delight of this succulent dish is that all the flavours are retained and accentuated by long, slow cooking inside the fluffy suetcrust wrap. Put the filling into the pastry-lined basin to within 2.5cm (1 in) from the top, no higher, and pour in the beef stock to cover the filling.

Dampen the pastry edges with water, then roll out the remaining suetcrust and place it on the filling, sealing the edges well. Cover securely, preferably with cooking foil. This should be pleated across the centre of the pudding to allow it to rise and tied securely with string. Tie a pudding cloth over it or use string to make a handle for lifting—either will serve the same purpose but a white cloth is, perhaps, more pleasing to the eye.

Have ready a pan of boiling water and put the pudding in, on an upturned saucer, so that the water is about half-way up the basin's side. Keep it at this level throughout the cooking, topping up when necessary with boiling water. Cook with a lid on the pan for 4 hours, then remove the lid, wrap the basin in a fine white cloth and serve immediately.

serves 6.

To make a Steak Pudding

mutton or beef steaks
1kg (2 lb) beef suet
1¾kg (4 lb) flour
salt and pepper

This recipe is one of Ann Peckham's, 1770.

'Take a quarter of flour, two pounds of beef suet shred fine, a little salt, mix them with water to a stiff paste, roll it of a moderate thickness; take mutton or beef steaks, season them with pepper and salt, make it up as yoy do an apple pudding tied up in a cloth; if it be a small pudding, two hours will boil it.'

serves 8.

MUTTON AND LAMB

Spiced Mutton

joint of mutton *or* lamb
cabbage *or* lettuce leaves
fine oatmeal
dripping *or* butter
1 cup cider
pinch of ground mace
thyme, chopped
black pepper

This is an old and popular method of cooking mutton in Yorkshire but is now often used for lamb.

Rub the joint well with a mixture of the oatmeal, chopped thyme, black pepper and mace. Dot the dripping or butter over the meat and wrap it in cabbage or lettuce leaves. Cook in a fairly slow oven until tender, and after the first 10 minutes of cooking pour the warmed cider into the tin and use this for occasional basting.

serves 4.

Breast of Mutton

breast of mutton
2 carrots, peeled and chopped
1 onion, cut up
stock
75g (3 oz) butter
fresh breadcrumbs
sprig of thyme
seasoning

Roll up the breast of mutton, fasten it, and put it into a pan with the peeled and chopped carrots and the prepared onion. Cover with stock, season and add the thyme. Bring to the boil, then cover and simmer for 1½ hours. Remove the meat, untie it and take out the bones, then weight and press until cold. Trim off any excess fat, cut into pieces and season. Melt the butter and dip each piece of meat into it, then into the breadcrumbs, and grill until crisp and golden brown on all sides. Serve with a spicy sauce.

serves 4.

Hodge Podge

best neck or scrag-end pieces of
    mutton *or* lamb
onions
carrots
turnips
celery
peas (optional)
beans (optional)
salt
pepper

This recipe was passed on to a woman living near Great Driffield by her aunt, whose family had farmed the area for generations. She herself used it regularly while her family lived at home.

Cover pieces of mutton or lamb with water and cook for 1 hour, skimming off any froth as it rises. Remove the meat from the pan and put in the prepared vegetables, especially carrots, turnips and celery, with peas and beans when possible, and always a large proportion of onions—perhaps as many as the rest of the vegetables together. Season and cook for 15 minutes, then season well (especially with pepper) and put in the meat. Cook together for a further 15 minutes by which time the hodge podge should be thick. Serve very hot.

Squab Pie

1kg (2 lb) best neck end of
   lamb
675g (1½ lb) dessert apples
4 small onions
150 ml (¼ pint) stock
grated rind of 1 lemon
shortcrust pastry *or*
   potatoes
1 level teaspoon cinnamon
large pinch of nutmeg
seasoning

Cut the meat from the bones and remove the skin. Cut into small pieces. Peel, core and slice the apples and peel and slice the onions. Grease a dish and put in the meat, apple and onion. Sprinkle in the spices and seasoning. Add the stock. Cover with pastry or a layer of potatoes, thinly sliced. Bake in a moderate oven 180°C (350°F), Gas Mark 4, for 1½ hours. If the pastry is getting too brown, cover with paper.

serves 6.

Mutton Pudding

675g (1½ lb) mutton
2 sheep's kidneys
1 onion, chopped
suetcrust pastry
stock
fresh herbs
seasoning

This traditional dish is rather fatty for present-day tastes but was popular in moorland and other areas of Yorkshire where sheep were raised. The suetcrust pastry with which the basin was lined was made using the fat from the sheep's kidneys.

Line a basin with the pastry, retaining enough for a cover, and add the cut up mutton and kidney, the chopped onion, seasoning and fresh herbs as preferred. Often wild thyme was used or perhaps a few rowan-berries might be added. Pour in stock until the basin is three-quarters full, then cover with a pastry lid. Steam the pudding, securely lidded, for 3 to 4 hours and serve piping hot with carrots and cabbage.

serves 4.

PORK

Pork Mittoon

equal amounts of:
sliced belly pork *or* bacon
and forcemeat *or* sausage meat
butter
ground mace
salt

This is an old country recipe and a version of the potted meats made in England for some centuries. Sheila Hutchins in *English Recipes* explains that a mittoon or mitton is a country version of the tureen. Tureen is a word once used to describe both the potted meats of the seventeenth century and the dishes which held them.

Butter a casserole or souflé dish very well and line with the pork or bacon. Add layers of forcemeat alternating with layers of pork or bacon until the dish is full. Season lightly with salt and ground mace on one or two of the layers. Top with pork or bacon, press down and cover. Bake in a moderately hot oven, 200°C (400°F), Gas Mark 6, for about 1 hour, and serve hot with mushrooms and brown gravy. Alternatively the mittoon can be pressed while hot and kept in a cool place to set overnight.

Potted Pork Roll

450g (1 lb) cooked minced
    pork
225g (½ lb) bacon
1 onion
100g (4 oz) softened butter
1 tablespoon tomato sauce
a good pinch of mace
seasoning

Fry the bacon until crisp, peel and chop the onion, and mix both with the minced pork. Season, add the ground mace, and mince all together. Beat in the sauce and softened butter and blend thoroughly. Pot and pour melted butter over the top.

serves 4.

HAM AND BACON

Boiled Ham

2kg (5 lb) ham
8 cloves
6 peppercorns
3 bay leaves
1 clove of garlic
breadcrumbs

Here is Mrs Gott's recipe, which was passed down to her from her great-grandmother.

Soak the ham overnight in cold water. Put into fresh water and boil for 5 minutes. Drain and again put the ham into clean water, adding the cloves, peppercorns, bay leaves and garlic. Cover and cook slowly for 3 hours or until tender. Leave to cool in the liquor, then skin and rub the fat over with browned breadcrumbs.

serves 10.

York Ham

York hams have been famous for many years and the original ones are said to have been smoked in the sawdust from oak used in the building of York Minster. These are large hams weighing between 7¼ and 10¾ kg (16 and 24 lb) and can be bought in York at any time of the year. They are cured in dry salt and lightly smoked.

Yorkshire Relish

575ml (1 pint) spiced vinegar
100g (4 oz) Barbados or
   Demerara sugar
50g (2 oz) salt
1 tablespoon treacle
2 tablespoons red chilli peppers
a good pinch of ground
   nutmeg

Yorkshire Relish is a traditional accompaniment to cold ham but is equally good with any cold meat.

Combine all the ingredients and bring slowly to the boil. Simmer for 5 minutes and allow to cool before bottling.

Yorkshire Sauce

1 orange
175ml (6 fluid oz) port
1 tablespoon brown gravy
1 tablespoon redcurrant jelly
a pinch of ground cinnamon

When ham is served hot, this sauce is an excellent accompaniment.

Cut the orange peel into fine strips without the pith and heat it in the port. Strain the liquor and stir in the gravy and redcurrant jelly. Reheat the mixture, adding the cinnamon and the juice of the orange, and serve hot.

Medley Pie

bacon
onion
1 dessertspoon chopped sage
apples
sugar
½ teacup water
shortcrust pastry

This recipe is taken from the manuscript book belonging to a farmer's wife from near Thirsk, who brought it up to date from a recipe book dated 1793 which belonged to her husband's family.

'Use enough slices of fat bacon to line a pie dish and cover with a good layer of sliced onion. Season and sprinkle on a dessertspoon of chopped sage. Peel and quarter some apples and put a thick layer of these in the dish with sugar to sweeten. Pour in half a teacup of water and cover the dish with a lid of shortcrust pastry. Bake in a moderate oven until the crust is nicely brown.'

OFFAL

Liver and Bacon Hot Pot

450g (1 lb) pig's liver
225g (½ lb) streaky bacon
1 large onion
1 large baking apple
breadcrumbs
stock and marjoram
herbs to taste, preferably
    parsley
seasoning

Cut the bacon and liver into small pieces and put a layer of liver into a greased dish. Cover with bacon and a sprinkling of breadcrumbs, herbs and sliced onion. Season and add a layer of apple. Repeat these layers until the dish is full, ending with breadcrumbs. Add warm stock or water, cover securely and bake in a moderately hot oven, 200°C(400°F), Gas Mark 6, for 1½ hours. Remove the lid and cook for a further 30 minutes to brown.

serves 4.

Tripe and Onions

675g (1½ lb) tripe
4 large onions
575ml (1 pint) milk
50g (2 oz) butter
25g (1 oz) flour
salt and pepper
nutmeg

Wash the tripe and cut it into small squares. Peel and slice the onions. Let them simmer together in the milk very slowly until tender, about 1 hour. Melt the butter, stir in the flour and cook for a minute before adding the milk from the tripe very gradually. Stir this sauce as it thickens, then add the tripe, onions and seasoning. Pepper and a pinch of nutmeg are excellent for the flavour. Heat thoroughly and serve with mashed potatoes.

serves 4.

Ox Tongue

1 ox tongue
jellied stock
2 carrots
2 onions
8 peppercorns
3 bay leaves

Tongue can be cooked fresh or, better still, after lying for a week to a fortnight in a pickle of salt, saltpetre and pepper. Ask your butcher's advice and he will probably pickle it for you. This recipe was given by Mrs Gott, who received it from her great-grandmother.

If the tongue is pickled, soak it overnight and then wash it. Place the tongue in fresh water with the carrots, onions, peppercorns and bay leaves. Bring to the boil and cook for 2 to 3 hours if fresh, or for up to 4 hours if pickled. Cook very gently until the tip is soft. Peel off the rough skin and any other unwanted bits, roll into a round, and put into a basin or cake tin. Pour in the stock before the tongue cools, cover with a plate, and press with a heavy weight overnight.

serves 6.

Oxtail Mould

1 jointed oxtail
225g (½ lb) bacon
1 onion
2 eggs
4 cloves
seasoning
stock

Peel the onion and stick with cloves. Put into a pan with the oxtail and bacon. Cover with water or stock and bring to the boil. Cover and simmer gently for 3 hours. Strain and reduce the liquid to 575 ml (a pint) or less. Remove the meat from the bones, then cut it and the bacon into small pieces and return to the pan with the reduced liquid. Boil the eggs until hard, then shell and halve. Place them with the cut sides towards the bottom of a greased basin. Bring the meat mixture to the boil and pour into the basin. Leave overnight in a cool place to set.

This kind of mould was very popular as a high tea dish and still features on farmhouse tea-tables.

serves 6.

Granny Brown's Brawn

450g (1 lb) shin of beef *or* pork
half a pig's head
1 onion
bunch of mixed herbs
blade of mace
2 cloves
10 black peppercorns
salt

This recipe for brawn is that used by Mrs Gott of Lothersdale, having been passed on to her from her great-grandmother.

Wash the pig's head thoroughly in salt water, scrape well and rinse. Put into a large pan with the beef and all other ingredients. Cover with boiling water, boil and skim. Simmer for 10 minutes and skim when necessary. Cover and simmer over a gentle heat for about 3 hours or until the meat leaves the bones easily. Remove all the bones and skin, and chop everything else together. Strain and check the seasoning, then put the meat into moulds. Boil up the stock with the bones, leaving off the lid to reduce and thicken. Pour a little of this stock into each mould. Leave in a cool place to set.

serves 4.

Poultry and Game

Poultry and Game

Until the end of the nineteenth century when game laws became more strict, all kinds of game were eaten in Yorkshire as elsewhere. Wild geese, curlews, coots and starlings were all considered fit for the table. Lark or heron puddings were served at banquets while cottagers were glad to eat anything that staved off hunger. Despite the cruel punishments meted out to anyone caught poaching, it was sometimes the only way in which a man could provide meat for his family. Rabbits were always prolific in Yorkshire's widespread moors and open fields, and were highly regarded until myxomatosis drastically culled the rabbit population some years ago. One old man told me that he remembered his mother paying ninepence each for rabbits when he was a boy, before the First World War. She cooked them in the oven by the fire with 'a lot of onion and a good rasher of home-cure [bacon] on top'.

The most common method of cooking young rabbits was simply to joint them, roll each piece in peppered flour, place knobs of butter on top, and then grill them. In this way the delicate flavour of the flesh predominates, whereas any addition of strong scented herbs might be overpowering. The bony pieces are never wasted by careful Yorkshire housewives who make a stock from them to use in rabbit pies. Older animals are used for pie-making, first being jointed, floured and fried, then placed in a casserole with carrots, peas, onions and mushrooms, chopped bacon and an optional cup of cider. Stock is poured in to cover the contents of the casserole and a layer of thick slices of potato is put in as topping. Alternatively the casserole can be partly cooked without potato then a thick pastry crust can be added and the dish returned to the oven until this is cooked.

An eighteenth-century recipe for rabbit recommended that rabbit joints be fried in butter and then stewed. A manuscript book belonging to another Yorkshire family of this period contained a typical recipe for roast hare. The hare was first stuffed with a 'pudding' or rich forcemeat made from the partially cooked, chopped heart, which was seasoned, spiced, mixed with breadcrumbs, finely chopped suet, chopped sweet herbs and cooked chestnuts, then bound with beaten egg and cream. After this the hare was roasted, thus making a banquet from what could be quite a humdrum beast if it was cooked without the creative love and knowledge of basic ingredients which typified the eighteenth century.

Yorkshire people also like to grill young hares. The joints are rolled in seasoned flour and lightly fried in butter. After placing them on a grilling rack hot milk is added to the butter in the frying pan and this mixture used to baste the grilling joints. This old method retains the flavour and moistness of the meat yet leaves each piece encased in a crisp, golden coating.

Old hares are treated like game and are hung unskinned for several days to develop the flavour and to tenderize the meat. They are then either stuffed with forcemeat and roasted whole, or jointed before cooking. The most common method in Yorkshire is to cook the joints on a rack set within an oven tin, basting frequently with melted butter. After cooking in a moderate oven for forty minutes, the juices are used to make gravy and the dish is served with traditional redcurrant jelly and bread sauce. A delicious variation has come from some families in the north-eastern part of the county who add a handful of small, whole mushrooms to the tin about ten minutes before the end of the cooking. The mushrooms become permeated with butter and the juices from the hare, making a superb accompaniment to the meal.

It is usual to hang all game birds, unplucked and ungutted, in a fairly cool place for between two and seven days depending on the species and the weather. A recommended test for readiness is to pluck the feathers just above the tail, and if they come out easily the bird is ready for cooking. One method of determining the age of game birds is to flex their feet and beaks which in young birds should be soft and pliable.

A medieval practice was to serve as a tracklement (accompaniment) any food the animal or bird might have lived upon. A 200-year-old recipe from Yorkshire involved the boiling of a pigeon in a rich stock after it had first been stuffed with barberries picked from the moors and hills. These were combined with chopped bacon and sweet herbs.

Grouse is often served stuffed with rowan-berries or the wild raspberries which can be found in the parts of Yorkshire inhabited by grouse. The roast grouse, brushed both inside and outside with melted butter before cooking, is sometimes presented without any stuffing other than a small whole onion, added to give moisture but not served with the meat. Two traditional accompaniments to grouse are a subtle, smoky jelly made from rowan-berries and a richer bilberry jelly.

Partridge is also sometimes cooked with an onion inside, and at least one Yorkshire family favours the old method of serving pheasant first brushed inside with melted butter then stuffed with a piece of steak and roasted. In this case the stuffing is to enrich the flavour, the steak being occasionally marinaded in red wine beforehand. These rich embellishments are admirable for game birds, but young pheasants are usually cooked like chickens and served simply with watercress. Gooseberry jelly is a popular accompaniment to pheasant, and gooseberries are also used in the traditional sauce to serve with goose.

Goose is even now more popular than turkey in country areas and has always been considered the festive fowl in Yorkshire. For centuries it was customary for goose to provide part of the rent handed to landlords on Michaelmas Day. From this custom arose the tradition of serving goose for dinner on this day, although legend links the practice with a later occurrence. The story is that Queen Elizabeth I was dining on goose one Michaelmas Day when news was brought to her of the defeat of the Spanish Armada. In commemoration of this victory goose became the traditional dish for that day.

Gargantuan game pies were made in Yorkshire during the Christmas festivities of the eighteenth century and featured impressively on banqueting tables. They were also sent as gifts to prominent people in London and records show that one was delivered to the Lord Chancellor from Sheffield in 1832. It unfortunately arrived late as the wagon carrying it broke down. This is not surprising when one considers the probable weight of these pies, each one containing a turkey, a goose, a hen or duck, a pigeon and any other small game fowl to be obtained. These were boned and stuffed one inside the next, all gaps being filled with forcemeat and hardboiled eggs, and the entire creation wrapped in a thick wall of pastry to form a container.

Although they have not been made for many years now, these pies could be regarded not as the blackbird pie of the nursery rhyme 'fit for a king' but as fit for a Yorkshireman, trencherman second to none.

POULTRY

Chicken Supreme with Fennel Sauce (Dales Style)

Chicken Supreme
the breast and wing from a
    chicken
50g (2 oz) grated Wensleydale
    cheese
1 beaten egg
flour
breadcrumbs

Fennel Sauce
25g (1 oz) flour
25g (1 oz) butter
575ml (1 pint) milk
50g (2 oz) ham, finely diced
a large pinch of fennel seeds
seasoning

This recipe comes from the Black Swan Hotel at Helmsley.
    Fillet the breast and wing. Cut a lengthwise pocket on each fillet and fold back. Stuff with cheese. Dip into the seasoned flour, egg wash, and breadcrumbs. Deep-fry gently until golden brown. Garnish the supreme with watercress or parsley.   Make a roux with the flour, butter and seasoning. Heat the milk and infuse the fennel seeds for 5 minutes. Strain the milk into the roux and cook to a double cream consistency. Add the finely diced ham and check seasoning. Serve the sauce separately with the chicken supreme.

serves 2.

Country Pot

1 plump chicken
225g (½ lb) bacon
1 onion
275ml (½ pint) light stock
fat
sweet herbs
seasoning
sweet white wine (optional)

Cut the chicken into joints. Chop the onion finely and fry in hot fat until golden, then put into an ovenproof casserole. Fry the bacon, sliced into small pieces, and put into the casserole with the joints of chicken. Add the stock and season well. Pour in a little sweet white wine if liked and a sprinkling of sweet herbs. Cover and cook in a slow oven 150°C (300°F), Gas Mark 2, until tender. This will take about 1½ hours.

serves 4

Chicken Rissoles

1 cooked breast of chicken
100g (4 oz) sausage meat
25g (1 oz) butter
25g (1 oz) flour

This recipe is unusual in that the 'rissoles' are enclosed in pastry.
    Mince the chicken breast with a little lemon peel. Pound it with the sausage meat and a good shake each of pepper and salt. Make a white sauce with the butter, flour and milk, and mix it into the

150ml (¼ pint) milk
shortcrust pastry
lemon peel
fresh breadcrumbs
pepper
salt

chicken mixture. Roll out the pastry thinly and cut into rounds. Put a spoonful of the chicken mixture on each round, dampen the edges, then fold over and seal. Press lightly into the breadcrumbs and fry until golden brown.

These rissoles must be sealed very carefully before frying, or alternatively they can be baked in a moderately hot oven.

serves 2

Boiled Turkey

1 turkey 6-7kg (12-14lb)
1 cooked calf's tongue
forcemeat or stuffing
450g (1 pint) of creamy white
   sauce
salt
10 black peppercorns
2 onions
2 sticks of celery
3 or 4 carrots
1 small turnip
vegetables to garnish—cooked
   peas and carrots

Stuff the turkey with the tongue and forcemeat or stuffing. Put it breast down in a large pan with the prepared carrots, turnip, celery and onions. Add salt, peppercorns and just enough cold water to cover. Bring to the boil then simmer, covered, for two hours or until tender. Keep the turkey hot, pour over the sauce and garnish with hot peas and carrots.

This old country method of cooking a turkey is still used in Yorkshire, the turkey being cooked breast down as it is when roasted. This keeps the juices in the meaty part of the bird. The quality of the sauce is important in this dish and often a proportion of single cream is used with the milk.

serves 10.

Wild Duck

Wild duck is served in Yorkshire farmhouses with a large nut of butter inside, well-seasoned and sometimes with a sprinkling of chives or finely chopped onion added to the butter. One family recommends putting a large spoonful of orange marmalade inside the cavity, another adds braised celery to the butter stuffing.

A Stuffing for Duckling

100g (4 oz) soft white
   breadcrumbs
50g (2 oz) raisins
50g (2 oz) chopped walnuts
1 stick celery
1 small onion
1 egg, well beaten
50 – 75ml (2 – 3 fluid ounces)
   milk

This recipe was given to me by a family living near Pontefract and is deliciously different.

Bring the milk to the boil and pour over the breadcrumbs. Peel and chop the onion finely, chop the celery and combine in a bowl with the walnuts, raisins and well-beaten egg. Stir into the breadcrumbs and milk, mixing well, and use to stuff a duckling.

Sauce for a Goose (Yorkshire 1769)

'Take the juce of sorrel, a little butter, and a few scalded gooseberries. Mix all together, and sweeten to your taste. You must not let it boil after you put in the sorrel, if you do it will take off the green. This is to be served separately.'

Gooseberry sauce was once the main accompaniment to goose but now it is more customarily served with mackerel. The method of making remains the same but the sorrel is omitted.

Buttered Grouse

1 brace of grouse
225g (½ lb) butter
2 blades mace
cayenne pepper
seasoning

Roast and joint the grouse and place in an oven dish. Add the butter to the juices and a little of the fat in which the grouse were roased. Grind the mace finely in a mortar or use an equal amount of ground mace. Season the butter, adding the mace and cayenne, and pour over the grouse joints. Serve when cold.

serves 2.

Grouse Casserole

1 brace of grouse
1 onion
1 carrot
2 tomatoes
100g (4 oz) mushrooms
50g (2 oz) melted butter
25g (1 oz) flour
575ml (1 pint) stock
seasoning

Prepare and joint the grouse and sprinkle with seasoned flour. Fry in the melted butter until brown then put into a casserole. Add the flour to the butter and stir over the heat until lightly brown, putting in a little more butter if necessary. Pour in the warmed stock, stirring well to avoid lumps. Bring to the boil and season to taste.

Skin and chop the tomatoes, onion and carrot finely and add to the casserole with the sliced mushrooms. Add the stock, cover and cook gently until tender, about 1½ hours.

serves 2.

Braised Guineafowl

1 guineafowl
225g (½ lb) chestnuts
1 large onion
some diced celery, to taste

Guineafowl has a pleasantly gamey flavour but is only rarely obtainable; perhaps increased demand from housewives who have sampled its unique quality will result in greater availability. The flesh can be a little dry but this is easily overcome by laying

100g (4 oz) butter
1 glass stock *or* red wine
seasoning

bacon rashers over the bird or by larding.

The guineafowl need not be jointed for braising but should first be lightly browned in 25g (1 oz) butter then placed breast down in a deep casserole. Dot with the rest of the butter, then surround with the onion cut into slices and some diced celery. Season and pour in the stock or red wine. Cover tightly and bake at 190°C (375°F), Gas Mark 5, for 45 minutes. Turn the bird breast upward, season, re-cover and cook for a further 30 minutes. Remove the lid and place the parboiled and peeled chestnuts around the bird. Return to the oven to brown the breast and cook the chestnuts. This should take about 15 minutes.

Carve and arrange the portions on a hot dish with the chestnuts. Check the liquid in the casserole for seasoning, pour over the bird and serve at once.

serves 2.

Roast Guineafowl

2 guineafowl
175g (6 oz) sausage meat
4 bacon rashers
3 tablespoons sweet sherry
25g (1 oz) brown breadcrumbs
50g (2 oz) parsley
seasoning
stock

Two guineafowl will serve six people lavishly. The stuffing should be made with good quality sausage meat—Cumberland sausages, with the skins removed, are ideal.

Blend the sausage meat and sherry. Season and mix in the breadcrumbs and finely chopped parsley. Stuff the birds and lay bacon rashers across the breasts. Roast on racks in a tin at 200°C (400°F), Gas Mark 6, for 1 hour and 10 minutes. Lift off the bacon, season the breasts and return to the oven to brown for a further 15 or 20 minutes. Use a good stock, preferably made from the giblets, to make gravy, together with the liquor left in the tin. Serve with bread sauce and any of the traditional accompaniments for pheasant—chestnuts, braised celery and potatoes.

serves 6.

Roast Partridge

Partridge is roasted for 20 to 25 minutes at a temperature of 220°C (425°F), Gas Mark 7, and served with bread sauce and gravy. Many Yorkshire families enjoy them cooked very simply. After being prepared they are put into a tin, covered with a rasher of fat bacon and cooked. Sometimes the birds are stuffed with either onions or mushrooms, which have been cooked until soft in butter.

Rolled Partridge

2 partridges
2 very thinly cut steaks
4 rashers streaky bacon
1 onion
good stock
sweet herbs
pinch of ground mace
salt
pepper

This is an eighteenth century recipe.

Chop the bacon and place half inside each bird. Sprinkle with salt, pepper, mace and chopped sweet herbs of your choice. Use the same blend of herbs to season the steaks. Place a bird in each steak, roll and tie round securely. Put the rolled partridges into an oven dish with some finely chopped onion and bacon. Add the stock, cover and stew gently until tender.

serves 2

Partridge Pudding

2 brace well-hung partridge
450g (1 lb) steak
100 – 175g (4 – 6 oz) Yorkshire
    ham, chopped
suetcrust pastry
stock to cover
25g (1 oz) flour
1 dessertspoon black pepper
1 dessertspoon of a mixture of
    salt, cayenne pepper and
    ground mace

Prepare the partridge and cut up. Line a greased basin with the pastry, about 1¼ cm (a half-inch) thick, setting some aside for a lid. Cover the sides and bottom of the basin with steak and season. Put the pieces of partridge into the centre together with the chopped ham, seasoning each layer and sprinkling with flour, then pour in stock to cover, and cover with pastry, then foil. Place on an upturned saucer in a pan of boiling water and steam for about 5 hours.

serves 6.

Supreme of Pheasant

1 pheasant
100g (4 oz) pâté
75g (3 oz) bacon
1 carrot, diced
1 onion, chopped
1 small tin apricots
1 egg
50g (2 oz) flour
dripping
breadcrumbs
275ml (½ pint) stock
2 tablespoons tomato purée
parsley
seasoning
1 measure brandy

This recipe is from the Black Swan Hotel at Helmsley.

Heat a little dripping, add all the flour and cook to a good brown colour. Add the tomato purée, the stock, finely chopped parsley and seasoning and bring to the boil. Fry the diced carrot and chopped onion, add to the stock and simmer for 2 hours. Strain. Purée most of the apricots, but hold back enough whole apricots to garnish. Add apricot purée to mixture.

Remove the supremes from the pheasants, i.e. the fillets of breast and wing in one piece. Season these, stuff with pâté and bind with bacon. Dip in flour, egg and breadcrumbs. Deep-fry gently. Present on a platter, garnished with apricots and watercress. Serve the sauce separately, adding the brandy just before serving.

serves 2.

To Stew Pigeons

pigeons
salt and pepper
cloves
sweet herbs
butter
1 litre (1 quart) good gravy
white wine
pickled mushrooms
peppercorns
3 – 4 blades of mace
lemon peel
onion
pickled oysters
extra butter
egg yolks
lemon for garnish

This is one of Hannah Glasse's recipes.

'Season your Pigeons with Pepper, Salt, Cloves, Mace, and some sweet Herbs; wrap this Seasoning up in a Piece of Butter and put in their Bellies; then tie up the Neck and Vent, and Half roast them; then put them into a Stew-pan with a Quart of good Gravy, a little White Wine, some pickled Mushrooms, a few Pepper Corns, three or four Blades of Mace, a Bit of Lemon-peel, a Branch of Sweet Herbs, a Bit of Onion, and some Oysters pickled; let them stew till they are enough, then thicken it up with Butter and Yolks of Eggs. Garnish with Lemon.
'Do Ducks the same way.'

Rabbit and Onions

1 rabbit
4 large onions
150ml (¼ pint) milk *or* single cream
25g (1 oz) butter
2 beaten egg yolks
1 teaspoon vinegar
1 bay leaf
thyme and parsley
seasoning
1 dessertspoon flour

Hannah Glasse gave a recipe using the combination of rabbit and onion, still highly popular in the north.

Cut the rabbit into joints and boil with two of the onions, peeled and chopped. Season the water before cooking and add to it the vinegar and herbs. Skim as necessary, simmer for about 40 minutes. Drain and sieve the stock.

Peel and chop the remaining two onions and cook in butter until soft. Remove the onions and stir a dessertspoon of flour into the butter. Gradually pour in the stock and stir while cooking for 5 minutes until thick. Take off the heat and stir in the beaten egg yolks and milk or cream. Keep warm but do not boil or the sauce will curdle. Add the onions and serve with the rabbit joints—traditionally the rabbit is covered in this onion sauce before serving.

serves 4.

Yorkshire Rabbit Pie

1 young rabbit
225g (½ lb) shoulder steak
175 – 225g (6 – 8 oz) cooked ham

Chop up the ham very finely and mix with a little sausage meat. Shape into balls. Prepare the rabbit, joint and roll in seasoned flour. Put the pieces into an oven dish. Cut up the steak and put into the dish with the ham balls. Season, add the finely chopped

100g (4 oz) sausage meat
1 onion, finely chopped
pastry
flour
stock
parsley, chopped
seasoning

onion and a sprinkling of chopped parsley. Pour in enough stock almost to cover the meat, put on an oven dish lid and bake in a fairly slow oven, 160°C (325°F), Gas Mark 3 for 1 hour or until tender. Remove the lid and cover with pastry, then bake in a hot oven till the pastry is cooked.

serves 6.

Rabbit Pudding

2 young rabbits
4 rashers streaky bacon
1 large onion, sliced
225g (½ lb) mushrooms
suetcrust pastry made from
   225g (½ lb) flour
flour
stock
sage
seasoning

Joint the rabbits and season. Line a greased basin with the suetcrust pastry but keep back enough for a lid. Cut the rashers of bacon into small pieces and put into the basin in alternate layers with the rabbit joints, the sliced onion, and the prepared mushrooms. Season the layers and sprinkle on a little flour and chopped sage. When all the ingredients have been added, pour in stock or water to within 2.5cm (1 inch) of the top and cover with the suetcrust topping. Put on a lid and steam for 3 hours.

serves 6.

Rabbit Brawn

1 large prepared rabbit
2 pig's trotters
herbs *or* spices
seasoning

Clean and joint the rabbit. Put the trotters into a pan, cover with water, and simmer for 1½ hours. Add the rabbit and cook for a further 2 hours. By this time the flesh should leave the bones easily. Cool slightly, remove all the bones and season with salt, pepper and herbs or spices such as parsley, sweet marjoram, cloves or ground mace. Cut the meat into neat pieces and bring back to the boil. Put into rinsed basins and leave overnight to set. Serve with salad for high tea.

serves 4.

Hare Jugged in Redcurrant Jelly

1 hare
450g (1 lb) redcurrant jelly
2 onions
seasoning
2 carrots
butter

Joint the hare and roll the pieces in seasoned flour. Fry in butter until brown, then put into a casserole. Add the redcurrant jelly, herbs and seasoning. Peel and slice the vegetables and put into the dish. Add two cloves before covering securely and putting the dish into a container of boiling water; then keep it simmering on the top of the cooker or in the oven for 3 to 3½ hours. Remove

serves 4.

1 bouquet garni
seasoned flour
2 cloves
cornflour

the joints to a hot dish, thicken the gravy with a little cornflour
and serve hot.

serves 4.

Venison

Perhaps more than any other meat, venison is evocative of the
countryside and retains a romantic and medieval association.
Because of this it can be doubly disappointing to find it carelessly
cooked.

A lean, somewhat dry meat, venison is best after marinading
(see below), then it can be roasted covered in fat bacon. Roast at
180°C (350°F), Gas Mark 4, for 30 minutes per 450g (1 lb), serve
with mushrooms, orange salad, rowan jelly or a venison sauce.

Venison Marinade

½ bottle red wine
150ml (¼ pint) oil
wine vinegar
1 onion
grated peel from half an orange
1 bay leaf
10 peppercorns, crushed
salt

Blend oil and red wine. Chop the onion finely and put with the
grated peel into the blended oil and red wine. Add a little wine
vinegar, the bay leaf, salt and crushed peppercorns. Heat very
gently but do not allow to boil, keep over the heat for 5 minutes,
then allow to cool.

To Make a Yorkshire Christmas Pye

This fantastic recipe was recorded by Hannah Glasse and is
typical of the pies sent from Yorkshire to London during the
eighteenth and even nineteenth centuries.

'First make a good standing Crust, let the Wall and Bottom be
very thick; bone a Turkey, a Goose, a Fowl, a Partridge and a
Pigeon. Season them all very well, take half an ounce of mace,
half an ounce of black pepper, all beat fine together, two large
spoonfuls of salt, and then mix them together. Open the fowls all
down the back, and bone them; first the pigeon, then the
partridge, cover them; then the fowl, then the goose, and then

the turkey, which must be large; season them all well first, and lay them in the crust, so as it will look only like a whole turkey; then have a hare ready, cased [skinned] and wiped with a clean cloth. Cut it to pieces; that is, jointed; season it, and lay it as close as you can on one side; on the other side woodcocks, moor game, and what sort of wild fowl you can get. Season them well, and lay them close; put at least four pounds of butter into the pye, then lay on your lid, which must be a very thick one, and let it be well baked. It must have a very hot oven, and will take at least four hours.

'This crust will take a bushel of flour . . . . These pies are often sent to London in a box as present; therefore the walls must be well built.'

Game Soufflé

225g (½ lb) cooked game
25g (1 oz) cooked ham
2 mushrooms
1 – 2 shallots, finely chopped
5 egg whites
4 egg yolks
100g (4 oz) butter
275ml (½ pint) warmed milk
6 dessertspoons flour
salt
cayenne and black peppers

Prepare a soufflé dish and preheat the oven to 200°C (400°F), Gas Mark 6. Put a baking sheet in the centre of the oven.

Melt 50g (2 oz) of the butter and stir in the flour, using just enough to make a firm but creamy roux. Cook gently for a few minutes, then stir in the warmed milk and beat until creamy. Take from the heat and beat in the egg yolks one at a time. Add the finely chopped game and ham, mushrooms and seasonings, using a good pinch of cayenne. Keep warm while frying the finely chopped shallots in the remaining butter until soft. Drain and stir into the game and ham mixture.

Whisk the egg whites until very dry and fluffy. Combine very gently with the game mixture then put into the prepared dish. Place on the tray in the oven and bake for 30 minutes. Serve immediately.

serves 4.

SAUCES FOR GAME

Savoury Game Jelly

1 cupful cooked game
4 oranges
1 onion, sliced
1 hard boiled egg
850ml (1½ pints) stock *or* water
4 teaspoons gelatine
a pinch of celery seeds
chives
watercress
seasoning

Simmer the stock with the sliced onion and celery seeds until reduced to 575ml (1 pint). Squeeze the juice from three oranges and soak the gelatine in this for 10 minutes. Pour the orange juice and gelatine mixture into the stock and stir until completely dissolved, then strain.

Chop the game into neat pieces and add with chives and seasoning to the stock. Rinse a mould in cold water and pour in about half a cupful of the stock, allow to set and cover with slices of hard-boiled egg. Pour on a little more stock and when this too has set add the game and rest of the stock to the mould. When completely set, turn out and garnish with watercress and slices of the remaining orange.

Orange Sauce for Game

2 oranges
25g (1 scant oz) of sugar
2 tablespoons port
425ml (¾ pint) stock
50g (2 oz) butter
25g (1 oz) plain flour
1 lemon (optional)

Peel the oranges thinly and without any pith. Cut the peel into strips and cook in water until just soft. Squeeze the juice from the fruit and add the sugar.

Make a roux with the butter and flour, bring the stock to the boil and add a little at a time, stirring continuously to avoid lumps. Cook for fifteen minutes then add the orange juice, peel and the port.

Lemon juice to taste can be added if liked to give a sharper flavour.

Harrogate Sauce

game juices
1 shallot, finely chopped
1 tablespoon mushroom ketchup
1 tablespoon lemon juice
a pinch of grated lemon rind
1 tablespoon boiling water
½ teaspoon powdered mace
pepper
1 wineglass claret

Put the juices from the game into a pan with the mushroom ketchup, boiling water, and lemon juice. Add the lemon rind and mace, the finely chopped shallot and a good shake of pepper. Simmer for 10 minutes and add the claret before serving.

Fish

Fish

Fish was an important item of diet in the past, for many days were prescribed as days of abstinence by the Church and Lent was strictly observed as a period of fasting. On such days, fish alone of animal flesh would be eaten. The relatively low cost of fish was another factor which contributed to the widespread popularity. A wide variety, mainly freshwater fish, was available, but as communications were appalling, large fish ponds known as 'stews' were built in the grounds of large houses to provide sources of fish. In 1467, when George Nevill was installed as Archbishop of York, the banquet menu included twelve 'porposes and Seales'. Medieval recipes used a strange variety of creatures under the term 'fish'.

On 27 February 1661 Samuel Pepys wrote in his diary: 'I called for a dish of fish, which we had for dinner, this being the first day of Lent; and I do intend to try whether I can keep it or no.' Next day he admitted: 'Notwithstanding my resolution, yet for want of other victuals I did eat flesh this Lent, but am resolved to eat as little as I can.'

All kinds of fish were sold in the markets of the sixteenth century and Leland wrote of Wakefield in this period: 'ys a very quik market toune, and meately large: wel servid of flesch and fisch both from the se and by ryvers, whereof dyvers be theraboute at hande, so that al vitaile is very good chepe there.'

One and a half centuries later a writer gave his account of Leeds: 'Above the market of the milk-cows, is the Ichthyopolium, which notwithstanding its great distance from the sea, is weekly twice or thrice, if not oftner, plentifully furnished with great variety of fish.'

All varities of freshwater fish were eaten. We have never since fully appreciated the qualities of carp or perch; grayling has a delicate flavour esteemed by many above the finest brown trout and is cooked similarly—simply baked in butter. One fisherman (anglers often like to cook their own catch) recommends wrapping each fish individually in cooking foil, first dotting the fish with butter and adding a small bay leaf to each package before baking.

Perch often formed the basis of an old English fish stew, 'water souchy', described as an equivalent to the Mediterranean *bouillabase*. There are examples of fish stews in every family recipe book of the eighteen century and Hannah Glasse gives a simple version of 'Water Sokey' in her book *The Art of Cookery Made Plain and Easy*, which is reprinted on page 68. Although many recipes favoured perch as the principal ingredient, the factors governing the composition of the dish were variety and economy; an angler's entire catch was included with no waste or rejections of species because of unsuitable flavour. A modern recipe is given on page 68.

Fish stews are being revived by hotels in Yorkshire, particularly those where a good selection of fish is available daily either from the sea or a river. A delicious dish created from a variety of fish is served at the Royal Hotel in Scarborough and the recipe appears on page 67. 'Water souchy' is possibly more closely allied with the fish chowders of New England. Perhaps a link could be made between the chowders of the early settlers of the New England states and 'water souchy', familiar to them from their native land.

Enormous amounts of dried fish were eaten in medieval days and Ling Pie was traditionally served on Good Friday at Filey from the dried salted ling prepared locally. An early account refers to ling being soaked in fresh water, then stewed in milk and butter which was sometimes thickened with eggs. This mixture was then eaten alone or in a pie which is a favourite of families living in Staithes. It was considered one of the local tests of good housewifery at the end of the last century for a girl to be able to make an acceptable Ling Pie, and Stanley Umpleby wrote of Staithes and this dish:

> *A dish fit for onny king*
> *Is yan o' them ling pies;*
> *Steeas women – an they're wise*
> *Knaws what ti deea wi' ling.*

We include a modern version of Ling Pie on page 64.

Another popular method of cooking ling is to coat it in fine oatmeal and then fry it with onions in butter. Then add finely chopped parsnips, herbs, seasoning and stock. Cover and bake slowly until the fish is tender. Solomongundy was also commonly made with boiled herrings and spices to serve as a Lenten or other fast day's dish. See page 81 for Hannah Glasse's recipe.

Potted fish has been made since Tudor times but has greatly declined in favour. Certain Yorkshire hotels whose chefs have been inspired by the English Tourist Board's eventual interest in regional foods, serve buttered or potted fish to perfection. Buttered crab, trout or salmon are easily prepared at home from perfectly fresh fish and are certainly worth the little effort. See pages 65 and 67 for some delicious recipes.

An unusual and delightful speciality of the Rose and Crown at Bainbridge is crayfish, rarely obtainable now but once plentiful in Yorkshire rivers. At their best they are simply boiled in salted water or white wine, garnished with parsley and eaten hot or cold.

Mackerel has been popular in Yorkshire for some centuries either potted or pickled, family recipe books also directing one to cook the fresh fish stuffed with fennel, then buttered and baked. Smoked mackerel can give a perfect start to a meal on its own or made into a paste. Easily obtainable in Yorkshire fishmongers it is not sold in anything like the amounts of wet fish.

Fish and chip shops also account for a high proportion of fish sales; these highly popular shops developed at the end of the last century when sea fish became more easily available everywhere. They are still plentiful but in nothing like the numbers that thrived sixty years ago. Old people vividly recall small shops, often set up in primitive wooden structures, hot and smelling of that favourite food of hungry children. Metal canisters of salt and vinegar in pop bottles on the counter are recollected; steaming, aromatic pans of 'black' peas bubbling on a gas ring to be measured into one's own basin. A considerate chip-shop owner might give a child pea-gravy and scraps (crispy batter pieces broken off the fried fish in cooking) free with his chips.

Cod was thought a 'most useful and excellent fish' with a soup to be made from the head, or the head and shoulders baked as a 'wholesome dish'. This followed the tradition of the previous centuries when nothing was wasted, fish bones and trimmings being used for stock, leftover pieces for pies. Fish cakes and kedgeree were popular breakfast dishes in Victorian days, admirable ways of using leftover fish, and fish cakes have retained their popularity in Torkshire. Two very good recipes are given on pages 69-70. Shellfish were common, especially oysters which were used in forcemeats, stuffings and stews. Local crab and lobster are served in hotels along the coast, and the Old Starre Inn at Bridlington is one of many to be recommended. With rapid transport it has become possible to buy shellfish all over the country and a traditional soup made from mussels is served at a restaurant in the cellars of the old Leeds Corn Exchange.

Another fish closely connected with the north is the silvery-gold kipper. The cure for herring was adapted from an older method by John Woodger of Northumberland but families in Yorkshire ports have been concerned with curing herrings for many years. The deep brown fish sometimes seen are the result of dyeing. Correctly cured herrings are smoked, preferably in oak sawdust, and have a tasty smoky-salt flavour. Slow grilling in butter is one well-liked method of cooking herrings or jugging in boiling water for ten minutes and serving with salad, brown bread and butter.

Now regarded as a luxury, salmon was once so plentiful in Yorkshire rivers that it was a commonplace item of food. The River Ure at Boroughbridge and the Ouse at York were famous for their salmon. Local methods of serving salmon are traditionally simple – poached or steamed in vinegar and water. See page 66 for a recipe. Baking was also popular in Yorkshire, recipes surviving from the mid-eighteenth century.

As can be expected from a county landing the heaviest catches of fish in England, Yorkshire markets supply an abundance of fresh fish and even in towns too small to hold a regular market there is inevitably an excellent fishmonger's shop where quality and choice is good.

FISH

Bloater Paste

3 large herrings
125g (5 oz) softened butter
3 teaspoons anchovy sauce
cayenne pepper
white pepper

Have a large pan of boiling water ready and plunge in the herrings to simmer for 10 minutes. Cut off their heads, then skin and fillet. Break up the fish and mix thoroughly with the softened butter, anchovy sauce, and cayenne and white peppers. This can be done in an electric blender.

serves 4.

Cod and Bacon

675g (1½ lb) of cod
2 rashers of bacon
1 large onion, sliced
100 – 175g (4 – 6 oz) cooked
    harricot beans (optional)
potatoes, thinly sliced
milk
parsley, chopped
seasoning

This is a typical north-eastern dish bearing a close resemblance to similar dishes common in New England coastal towns.

Cut the fish into pieces. Butter an oven dish and cover the bottom with sliced onion. Put a layer of fish over the onion, season and add a sprinkling of chopped parsley. Chop the bacon and use half to place over the fish. Cover with the beans if desired. Repeat these layers until all the ingredients are used. Pour on milk to come level with the top layer and cover with thin slices of potato as required. Bake in a moderately hot oven, 200°C (400°F), Gas Mark 6, until tender, about 40 minutes.

serves 4.

Steamed Gurnet

This large-headed ugly fish has nevertheless a good flavour, and a popular method of cooking the prepared fish is to steam it gently, then either pour melted butter over it or serve with a parsley sauce. This method is preferred by older people but young housewives have told me that they like to present the fish rather more elaborately, perhaps as an antidote to its unattractive appearance.

Stuffed Gurnet

1 gurnet
1 slice brown bread
25g (1 oz) butter
1 egg yolk
milk
anchovy essence to taste
thyme, chopped
marjoram, chopped
ground nutmeg
salt
pepper
1 slice bacon

I was given this recipe in Bridlington by a young housewife who is married to a deep-sea fisherman.

Moisten the brown bread in milk. Squeeze it out and beat it with the butter, chopped thyme and marjoram, and season it well with salt, pepper and a pinch of ground nutmeg. Add anchovy essence to taste and bind the mixture with egg yolk. Stuff the gurnet and place on a piece of buttered cooking foil, top with a slice of bacon and wrap the fish securely but not too tightly. Bake in a moderately hote oven 200°C (400°F), Gas Mark 6, for 30 minutes, and serve with anchovy sauce.

serves 1.

Grilled Haddock

This firm-fleshed fish is usually prepared and cooked very simply along the east coast, where the cleaned and gutted fish is often grilled. Butter is dotted over first and when this has melted flour is sprinkled over to give a crisp surface. The fish is grilled for about 6 minutes on each side. A favourite sauce to serve with grilled haddock is shrimp sauce.

Another method of cooking is to grill as before until the butter has melted and then brush with beaten egg, sprinkle with flour and again dot with butter before continuing to cook the fish.

Stuffed Haddock

1 haddock
100g (4 oz) fresh breadcrumbs
50g (2 oz) shredded suet
1 shallot
1 egg
1 teaspoon finely chopped
    parsley
1 teaspoon finely chopped
    thyme
pinch of ground nutmeg
seasoning

Combine the breadcrumbs, suet, egg and the finely chopped shallot. Add the herbs, nutmeg and seasoning. Stuff the mixture into the prepared haddock. Steam the fish until tender and serve with egg sauce.

serves 2.

Creamed Haddock

3 haddock fillets
75g (3 oz) butter
flour
1 breakfast-cup mixed milk and
  cream
1 teaspoon made mustard
seasoning

Roll the fillets of haddock in seasoned flour. Melt the butter in a frying pan and lightly brown the fish on both sides in the butter. Pour in the milk and cream mixture, bring to the boil, and cook for 1 minute before lowering the heat and simmering, covered, until tender. Lift out the fish carefully and add the mustard to the pan—a generous teaspoon or according to taste. Boil this liquid until thick then pour over the fish to serve.

serves 3.

Baked Halibut or Cod

1 halibut or cod steak
1 onion, sliced
butter
6 slices lemon
2 bay leaves
1 glass white wine

Gently fry the sliced onion until soft and place in a buttered oven dish. Cover with the fish and lay the lemon slices on top. Season, add the bay leaves and dot with butter. Put into a moderately hot oven for 7 or 8 minutes then add the white wine, cover, and continue baking for a further 30 minutes or until cooked.

serves 2.

Kipper Paste

2 kippers
50 g (2 oz) butter
a squeeze of lemon juice
black pepper

Steam two kippers and remove all the bones. Beat or mince the flesh with the softened butter, black pepper and lemon juice. Serve freshly made with toast.

serves 6.

Baked Whiting

2 whitings
1 onion, sliced
50 g (2 oz) butter, melted
125-275ml (¼-½ pint)
   white fish stock *or* milk
lemon juice
1 dessertspoon parsley,
   chopped
grated nutmeg
salt
pepper

This is an old Yorkshire recipe.

Butter a baking dish and sprinkle with chopped parsley, then sliced onion and a little grated nutmeg. Place the prepared whitings in the dish, pour a little melted butter over them and some fish stock or milk. Add salt to taste, put into a moderately hot oven and when half-cooked turn them carefully. When they are ready pour the juice into a pan, add some butter and slowly bring to the boil. Add a few drops of lemon juice and a little pepper. Pour over the fish and serve.

serves 2.

Soused Herring

450g (1 lb) herring
2 onions, sliced
mixture of ⅔ vinegar and ⅓
    water
1 bay leaf
6 peppercorns
2 or 3 whole allspice
2 cloves *or* 2 sprigs parsley
seasoning

Wash and scrape the herring, trim and split lengthwise. Remove the bones, season and roll up, halved along the spine if the fish are large. Put them into a buttered dish with the bay leaf and sliced onions on top. Season and add the peppercorns, allspice, cloves or parsley, and liquid to cover. This should be two-thirds vinegar to one-third water. Cover and bake in a slow oven for 1 hour then remove the lid and continue cooking until the fish is tender. Serve when cold with lemon slices to garnish.

serves 4.

Herring Pie

2 herrings
2 parboiled potatoes
1 baking apple
1 onion
butter
½ cup water
parsley
salt

Clean and bone the herrings, quarter and rub with salt. Thinly slice the potatoes and thickly cover the base of a buttered oven dish with some slices. Wash the fish and place half over the potato. Slice the apple, use half to cover the fish and sprinkle on finely sliced onion and chopped parsley. Season and repeat these layers, topping with potato and knobs of butter. Pour in the water, cover, and bake in a moderate oven, 180°C (350°F), Gas Mark 4, for 30 minutes. Remove the lid and cook for a further 15 minutes until tender and brown.

serves 2.

Ling Pie

450g (1 lb) ling
175 g (6 oz) bacon
½ onion, finely chopped
2 eggs
275 ml (½ pint) milk
flour
salt
pepper
shortcrust pastry

Cut the ling into slices and place in a buttered dish. Sprinkle with salt, pepper, flour and the finely chopped onion. Hard-boil the eggs, slice and lay over the fish. Cut up the bacon and add to the dish, then pour in the milk. Cover with a lid of shortcrust pastry and bake at 180°C (350°F), Gas Mark 4, for 1 hour.

serves 4.

Potted Salmon

450g (1 lb) salmon
100g (4 oz) butter, slightly
  softened
ground mace *or* anchovy
  essence
allspice
ground black peppercorns
seasoning

Fillet and break up the salmon, put into a basin with the slightly softened butter and season to taste with salt, ground mace or anchovy essence, ground black peppercorns and allspice. Cover and place over a pan of boiling water to cook. Once the salmon is hot this will take about 15 to 20 minutes. Take the pan from the heat but leave the basin where it is until cool. Stir the salmon well and put into pots. When quite cold cover with clarified butter.

serves 4.

Salmon with Cucumber

2 or 3 salmon steaks
50g (2 oz) butter
1½ lemons
1 tablespoon white wine
salt
½ cucumber
parsley, finely chopped

Salmon is at its best when served simply, the Yorkshire preference being to poach it and serve it with a little of its own juices or melted butter. This old Yorkshire recipe is based upon the affinity between salmon and cucumber.

Butter an oven dish well and place the salmon steaks in it. Add the butter, the strained juice of one lemon and the wine. Sprinkle lightly with salt and cover with a sheet of buttered greaseproof paper. Bake in a moderately hot oven for 20 minutes. Peel the cucumber and cut into chunks. Lightly steam it and mix gently with finely chopped parsley and a few squeezes of lemon juice. Serve the steaks very hot with the cooking liquid poured over them, and garnished with the cucumber.

serve 2-3.

Spiced Salmon

675g (1½ lb) salmon
1 onion
mixture of ⅔ wine vinegar to
    ⅓ water
1 dessertspoon black
    peppercorns
3 cloves
a pinch of ground cinnamon
seasoning

Cut the salmon into pieces and place in a dish with the cloves, cinnamon, peppercorns, and seasoning, the sliced onion and enough wine vinegar and water to cover. Use twice as much vinegar as water. Poach the salmon by bringing the liquid to the boil and then simmering for 15 minutes. Remove the skin and leave in a cool place overnight. Serve cold or reheat gently if preferred.

serves 4.

Bechemele of Fish

450 g (1 lb) pike, cod or skate
    (boned)
275 ml (½ pint) cream
1½ spoonfuls anchovy liquor
    or essence
1 teaspoonful mustard
1 teaspoonful ketchup
pepper
flour
butter
breadcrumbs

This is from a manuscript cookery book in the Blanche Leigh Collection, Brotherton Library, University of Leeds (MS. 60, dated 1825).

'Pike, Cod or Skate pick them from the bones. To one pound of this add ½ pint cream, 1½ spoonful of Anchovy liquor or Essence, 1 teaspoonful good mustard, 1 do Catsup, pepper to your taste. When nearly hot add a little flour and butter—make it quite hot and put it in a dish then strow bread crumbs over it—baste it with butter till the crumbs are quite moist—then salamander it.'

A salamander, which was a cast-iron plate, was made hot and passed over the top of a dish to brown it. In present day kitchens, grilling would have the same effect.

Buttered Crab

1 boiled crab
50g (2 oz) softened butter
1 tablespoon cream
1 tablespoon breadcrumbs
2 tablespoons white wine
1 anchovy fillet (optional)
a pinch of nutmeg
salt
pepper
parsley

This is adapted from an eighteenth-century recipe.
    Flake the edible meat from a boiled crab and mix with the softened butter, salt, pepper, and nutmeg. Add the breadcrumbs, cream and wine. A pounded anchovy fillet can also be added at this point. Blend thoroughly and put in the cleaned crab shell, dot with butter and grill for 10 minutes. Garnish with parsley and serve with hot buttered toast.

serves 4.

Buttered Lobster

1 freshly boiled lobster
50g (2 oz) unsalted butter
a pinch of salt
a pinch of cayenne pepper
a pinch of white pepper
melted butter
parsley

Crack the lobster's claws, quarter the shell and remove all the meat. Pound this with the butter, salt, and peppers. Replace in the cleaned shell pieces, brush with melted butter and bake in a hot oven, 230°C (450°F), Gas Mark 8, until browned. Serve hot and garnished with parsley.

serves 6.

Scarborough Coble Stew

mussels
prawns
fresh filleted fish if possible to
    include: monk, woof, skate
    knobs, rock salmon—but
    any fairly solid fish if these
    are not available
streaky bacon, chopped
onions
raw potatoes
flour
a little double cream
a little white wine
chopped parsley
salt and pepper
oil
light fish stock to cover

This recipe comes from the Royal Hotel, Scarborough.
    Fry chopped bacon in a little oil to extract the fat, then add chopped onion and fry slowly without browning. To this add flour to form a roux and cook for a few minutes; then add the potatoes, peeled and chopped into 2½ cm (one inch) dice, moisten with a little white wine and light stock or water to bring to the consistency of single cream. Bring to the boil, add the fish cut into 2½ cm (one inch), pieces and cook for approximately 20 minutes, stirring occasionally. The prawns and mussels should be added about 5 minutes before the end of the cooking time. Remove from the heat and stir in a little double cream and finish with parsley. Serve in soup bowls with water biscuits offered separately.

Hannah Glasse's Sokey

'Take some of the smallest Plaice or Flounders you can get, wash them clean, cut the fins close, put them into a Stewpan, put just enough Water to boil them in, a little Salt and a Bunch of Parsley, when they are enough, send them to the Table in a Soop-Dish, with the Liquor to keep them hot. Have Parsley and Butter in a Cup.' (1747)

Water Souchy

4 large perch *or* an assortment
   of freshwater fish
225g (½ lb) carrots
1 leek
50g (2 oz) butter
2 tablespoons chopped parsley
bouquet garni
salt and pepper

An eighteenth-century recipe similar to Hannah Glasse's used perch cooked in salted water with a little milk added. Sliced onion and chopped parsley were usually included and perch has always been preferred although whatever the angler caught would be used.

Make a stock from the cleaned and chopped carrots, the leek and the fish bones, skin and trimmings. Clean the fish and cut into chunks. Put into a pan with the butter, herbs, seasoning and stock and bring to the boil, then simmer until just tender. Do not overcook and serve hot.

serves 6.

Fish Pot

fish
onions
mashed potato
seasoning

A fish pot was a common enough dish in fishing ports and this fish pie from Whitby appears to be an adaptation of the traditional dish. Made from any variety of fish left on the quay, perhaps damaged and given away but sometimes taken by old fish-wives who then hawked them around the streets near the harbour, fish pots were still being made regularly in one household in Whitby according to the old method until about fifteen years ago.

This recipe is a classic example of almost peasant cooking at its best, using whatever basic ingredients are available in a method designed to bring out their finest qualities within the constraints imposed by poverty, lack of equipment, etc.

Grease a deep dish with good fat and into it put any fish available and some onions cut into thick slices. Cover with a tight lid and bake until the fish is tender. Remove the skin, bones, etc., and flake the fish. Season well and mix with hot mashed potato then put back into the oven without a lid to brown.

Simple variations can be made with the addition of herbs or sliced tomatoes, peas and tomato purée or cheese. Tomato sauce is a good accompaniment.

Shrimp Savoury

575ml (1 pint) prepared
    shrimps
5 large tomatoes
75g (3 oz) butter
75g (3 oz) breadcrumbs
1 dessertspoon sugar
salt
pepper

Skin the tomatoes by plunging them into boiling water and leaving them for a few minutes when the skins will peel away quite easily. Cut off the soft flesh of the tomatoes, discarding the cores, and put this into a pan with the butter, salt, pepper, and sugar. Simmer until a creamy consistency is reached, then stir in the breadcrumbs, keep some for the topping, and bring to the boil. Add the prepared shrimps and cook for 3 minutes. Put into a buttered pie dish and top with a sprinkling of breadcrumbs. Bake in a moderately hot oven for 10 minutes and serve hot.

serves 6.

Fish Scallops

white fish
potatoes
batter

Fish scallops can be bought already cooked in many of the fish and chip shops in Yorkshire but they are also very popular as a home-made dish, especially in families with children.

Hold a slice of firmly fleshed white fish—cod is ideal—between two slices of peeled potato and dip into the batter. Deep-fry this sandwich for 10 minutes and serve with vinegar or home-made tomato sauce. Several of these scallops are made at the same time and, depending on size, 3 or 4 make one serving.

Whitby Fish Pie

450g (1 lb) white fish
100g (4 oz) lean raw ham
2 hard-boiled eggs
butter
black pepper
seasoning
shortcrust pastry

Steam the fish, flake and remove all bones. Cut up the ham and slice the hard-boiled eggs. Butter an oven dish generously and fill with alternate layers of the three ingredients. Moisten with a little of the liquor from the fish, season and add a good sprinkle of freshly ground black pepper. Cover with shortcrust pastry and bake in a moderate hot oven until the pastry is golden brown.

serves 6.

Traditional Fish Cakes

450g (1 lb) cooked fish
225g (½ lb) mashed potatoes
25g (1 oz) butter

Flake the fish and combine with the potato, parsley and butter. Separate the egg and beat the yolk into the mixture, season and form into rounds. Dip into the seasoned flour and then into the

1 egg
breadcrumbs
seasoned flour
chopped parsley
salt and pepper

egg white which has been beaten. Finally, roll in the breadcrumbs and fry on both sides in hot fat until golden.

serves 6.

Fish and Oatmeal Cakes

1½ teacups cooked fish
3 teacups cooked oatmeal
½ onion, finely chopped
50g (2 oz) butter
1 tablespoon chopped parsley
seasoning
egg
breadcrumbs

Have ready the cooked oatmeal and cooked fish. Melt the butter and in it fry the finely chopped onion until soft. Combine the onion, fish and oatmeal, season well and add the parsley. Shape into flat cakes and dip into beaten egg, then breadcrumbs. Fry in hot fat until lightly browned.

serves 6.

Fish Pudding

450g (1 lb) cooked white fish
2 eggs, beaten
50g (2 oz) butter, softened
75g (3 oz) fresh breadcrumbs
finely chopped parsley
milk
cream (optional)
seasoning

Flake the fish, removing any bones, and mix with the beaten eggs, finely chopped parsley, softened butter and breadcrumbs. Season well, adding freshly ground black pepper. Beat in enough milk to give a soft dropping consistency and use cream intead of some milk if this is available. Butter a basin, fill with the mixture, cover and steam for 1 hour. Serve with peas or green beans and sauté potatoes.

serves 6.

Soups, Vegetables, Salads and Savouries

Soups, Vegetables, Salads

This section covers a very wide field indeed and Yorkshire people have been especially fond of savoury dishes, one confirmation being the interest shown in Mrs Gott's Spring Salad (page 83) and Granny Brown's Brawn (page 40) at the country teas in Lothersdale.

Soups are most favoured in Yorkshire when simple and single-flavoured like watercress, kidney or chicken, but a sturdy country-vegetable soup is always appreciated. For a selection of Yorkshire soup recipes see pages 76 and 77.

Vegetable dishes and salads have the greatest appeal when served with a hearty savoury or main course meal. On the whole the trenchermen of Yorkshire prefer their vegetables lightly cooked and simply presented. During the eighteenth century, England had a fine reputation for cooking vegetables although John Farley warned in 1783 (*The London Art of Cookery*) that: 'Numbers of cooks spoil their Garden Stuffs by boiling them too much. All kinds of vegetables should have a little crispness, for if you boil them too much you will deprive them both of their sweetness and beauty.'

Early in the eighteenth century Richard Bradley wrote that 'Parsnips, Carrots, Turnips, Skirrets, Scorzonera, Beets, Radishes, Horseradish, Jerusalem Artichokes, Onions, Leeks and their Kinds' were in common use. The value of herbs was better understood then than at any period since and sorrel, garlic, shallots, truffles and globe artichokes feature regularly on the tables of the wealthy.

Potatoes have long been common in Yorkshire, the north of England excelling in the cooking of this vegetable. One favourite Yorkshire method is to bake them in their skins and a very popular tea-time dish is potato cakes, any left uneaten being fried next morning with the breakfast bacon.

Parsnips were more popular in the past than at present, mashed parsnips once being considered as traditional a part of Sunday dinner as the roast beef and Yorkshire pudding. Hannah Glasse recommended boiling the parsnips till soft, then draining them and scraping off the skins and 'with a knife scrape them all fine, throwing away all the sticky Parts; then put them into a Sauce-pan with some Milk, and stir them over the Fire till they are thick. Take great Care they don't burn, and add a good Piece of Butter and a little Salt, and when the Butter is melted send them to table.' A very similar method of cooking parsnips prevails to the present day in the north of England.

Before the Victorian era when a tendency developed to cook vegetables to a placid mush, vegetable cooking was carried out with style and economy.

and Savouries

Ann Peckham of Leeds, 'well known to have been for Forty Years one of the most noted cooks in the county of York', gave methods of cooking vegetables in *The Complete English Cook (1767),* which resulted in imaginative dishes of the type Yorkshire people have enjoyed ever since. Peas were cooked in butter with chopped lettuce, onions and seasoning, celery or red cabbage was lightly stewed and served with a simple dressing and readers were advised to cook 'all sorts of sprouts and cabbages with seasoned water but to be strained when stalks are tender, drained and served with butter.'

Another writer of the period gave a recipe for a 'grateful winter sallet' in which the 'roots of the red beet' were boiled, sliced when cold and covered in a dressing of 'oil, vinegar, salt, etc.'—a method still popular in many Yorkshire farmhouses.

Salads have never been accepted with much enthusiasm in Yorkshire unless substantial in themselves or as an accompaniment to a meal; Solomongundy is typical of the robust salads which have survived for centuries. A recipe of 1741 uses six prepared, boiled herrings, the flesh being taken from the bones to leave the skeleton and head intact then chopped with four anchovies, a large diced onion, some capers, chopped mushrooms, a few pickled oysters and the grated rind of two lemons. This mixture is placed over the bones in the form of a fish and garnished with lemon slices, capers, oysters and mushrooms.

Hannah Glasse gives a Solomongundy recipe for Lent which uses apples, celery, hard-boiled eggs, cucumber, red cabbage and pickled herrings while Ann Peckham's recipe for Solomongundy (page 81) uses chicken or veal and beef or tongue as the main ingredients for the dish and is the type of mixture still enjoyed for high tea in Yorkshire.

Many Yorkshire savoury dishes are peculiar to the north, often to the county. Pig's trotters, pease pudding (see page 86), faggots, harslet, tripe and black pudding (see page 85) are traditional and localized. Faggots are sometimes known as savoury ducks and are made all over England. Variations occur but they were originally a tasty method of using up the heart, lights and any scraps of pork left over from pig-killing.

One dish which is synonymous with Yorkshire yet which raises constant discord over methods of preparation is Yorkshire pudding. Some say that the reason for the pudding being customarily served with gravy before the meat course is an economic one, since the more pudding they eat the less beef the family will then consume. An elderly farmer's wife was indignant at this suggestion, explaining that in her family the pudding was served quickly and first, being so light that the family had to sit round the table poised in readiness for the instant that the pudding was cooked. Any delay results in a 'flopped pudding', her belief being that 'the rubbery squares dished-up in a lot of restaurants as Yorkshire pudding come from too cool an oven and too long a wait before serving.' Three Yorkshire pudding recipes are to be found on pages 83-84.

The enthusiasm generated by Yorkshire people over a dish of black pudding or tripe results in a very high standard of product indeed. Tripe is carefully chosen for serving cold, well salted and with lashings of vinegar, or steamed with onions in white sauce (see page 39 for recipe). Black puddings are usually heated in hot water then served with mustard and bread and butter. In many homes the preference is to slice and grill them as an accompaniment to bacon and eggs. This is a great favourite at breakast-time in many rural areas. Some families prefer them served with boiled and mashed potatoes, carrots, and onion sauce, while a combination of two typical and traditional north-country delicacies is black puddings and oatcakes.

Highly localized is the Dock Pudding traditionally served at Eastertime in the Calder Valley area. Surviving from days when sweet dock, *Polygonum bistorta*, was among the earliest of green vegetables to grow in the spring and was picked as a refreshing change from the dry salt foods of winter, dock pudding is still considered beneficial by old people who describe it as 'a right good blood-cleanser'. Whole families still go out to pick docks in Mytholmroyd, Hebden Bridge and Heptonstall; dock pudding is so much enjoyed that some women now freeze cartons of it to eat with their Christmas dinner. For a short season it is possible to buy jars of the pudding, sold to raise money for the Calder Valley Junior Band.

One 76-year-old who still goes out to gather her own docks to make the dish told me that 'dock pudding keeps you young, keeps your mind active'. She also explained that her grandson, when offered bacon and eggs for breakfast, suggested that 'it would be even better with some dock pudding'. A contemporary of hers described to me her method of making this old dish:

I put about a pound of onions to as many docks as I can think—about three or four pound. I allus gather mine by t'canal. Not much water in mind, if your pudding's sloppy it'll put you off for evermore. I puts a good knob of butter in and salt, but you can never gauge t'salt—have to keep tasting. Then keep chopping as it's cooking. I make mine in t'old iron pan. Cook 'em for three or four hours till they're right tender and as it boils down keep putting more in. Then sprinkle oatmeal in for t'last ten minutes. My niece puts eggs in but I don't think much to that.

Children gather docks for grandmothers and great-grandmothers who are still anxious to make the dish but no longer able to go out picking their own leaves. Younger women also continue the tradition for their families and take jars of pudding to older relatives. One explained that her uncle was unappreciative of dock pudding: 'Auntie Florrie makes it but me uncle throws it on t'muck midden when her back's turned.' From the shocked chuckles that greeted this comment I gathered that 'uncle' was a rarity in this district of dock pudding gourmets.

SOUPS

Kidney Soup

100g (4 oz) beef kidney
100g (4 oz) shin beef
1 small onion
2 carrots (finely chopped)
2 tablespoons barley
2 level tablespoons cornflour
2 litres (3½ pints) stock
finely chopped parsley
1 bay leaf
nutmeg
seasoning

Chop the beef and kidney finely and brown in melted butter or fat. Chop the onion finely and fry until soft then put it into a pan with the meats, the finely chopped carrots and the stock. Season, adding a bay leaf and a pinch of nutmeg if liked. Add the barley and bring to the boil slowly, then cover and simmer for two hours. Purée, add the cornflour blended with a little cold water, and again cover to cook for a further 15 minutes.

serves 8.

Chicken Broth

1 boiling fowl
1 onion
1 carrot
1 leek
1 small stick celery
½ small turnip
25g (1 oz) rice *or* barley
blade mace
seasoning

Cut the chicken into small pieces, break the bones and put chicken and bones into a pan. Cover with water, bring to the boil and skim. Cover and simmer for almost 3 hours. Season and strain the liquid. Prepare all the vegetables and cut into neat pieces. Add to the chicken liquid in the pan, together with the rice or barley and a piece of blade mace. Cover and simmer until tender, between 20 and 30 minutes.

serves 6.

Hare Soup

1 large hare
3½ litres (3 quarts)
    water
1 onion
white peppercorns
salt
mace
2 spoonfuls soya sauce *or*
    3 spoonfuls mushroom *or*
    walnut ketchup
cayenne pepper
2¼ litres (2 quarts) gravy
275ml (½ pint) red wine

This recipe is taken from the same 1804 cookbook as the Vegetable Soup on page 78. The writer has commented: 'to speak in praise of this stew, would be a eulogium on the gout.'

'Cut a large hare into pieces, and put it into a stew pan, with three quarts of water, one onion, a few corns of white pepper, a little salt and some mace. Stew over a slow fire for two hours, or till it becomes a good gravy. Then cut the meat from the back and legs, and cut it to put into the stew when nearly ready. Put the bones into the gravy and stew till the remainder of the meat is nearly dissolved. Then strain off the gravy, and put to it two spoonfuls of soy, or three of mushroom or walnut catchup. Cayenne pepper to the taste. To two quarts of gravy put half a pint of red wine. Then put in the meat that was cut off from the back and legs and let the whole boil about a quarter of an hour. Send it hot to the table.'

Game Soup

450g (1 lb) remains of any
   type of game
1 carrot
1 large onion
stock to cover
3 cloves
1 or 2 bay leaves
chopped parsley
ground mace
black pepper
salt and pepper
100g (4 oz) uncooked beef
sherry (optional)

Prepare and chop the carrot and onion and put them into a pan with the cut up pieces of game, bay leaves, chopped parsley, cloves and seasoning. Add a pinch of ground mace and black pepper and cover with a good stock. Bring to the boil then simmer, covered, for 2 hours. Strain the liquid and return to the boil. Put in a few pieces of raw beef, boil, then strain again after a few minutes. A little sherry can be added before serving.

serves 6.

Lobster Soup

225g (8 oz) remains of cooked
   lobster
1 onion
1 stick celery
¼ cucumber
100g (4 oz) peas
100g (4 oz) spinach (if
   available)
anchovy essence
stock

Melt the butter and in it fry the chopped onion until soft. Add all the other vegetables, suitably prepared, and cook until soft. Purée and return to the pan. Season, then add the stock, lobster, and anchovy essence to taste. Heat gently and serve hot.

serves 4.

Watercress Soup

a bunch of watercress
1 large potato
50g (2 oz) bacon
850ml-1 litre (1½-2
   pints) stock
150ml (¼ pint) single cream

Peel and chop the potato and put into a pan with the cleaned watercress broken into small pieces. Lightly fry the bacon and add to potato and watercress mixture with the stock. Bring to the boil slowly, then simmer for approximately 1½ hours until tender. Season, sieve or purée, and reheat. Stir in the cream just before serving and sprinkle with chopped watercress leaves.

serves 4.

Vegetable Soup

stock for gravy soup (beef stock)
175g (6 oz) butter
6 onions
6 heads of celery
2 handfuls spinach
2 cabbage lettuce
1 handful sorrel
4 carrots
4 turnips
extra butter
flour
575ml (1 pint) green peas (in
    season)
salt and pepper

An observation made after this 1804 recipe had been written stated: 'This dish is only proper for those who do not stand in fear of gouty shoes and a pair of crutches'.

'Have ready the stock for gravy soup. Put six ounces of butter into a stew pan, and melt it till it has been hissing. Have ready six onions cut, throw them in and shake well. Boil for five or six minutes, then put in six heads of celery, cut small, two handfuls of spinage, two cabbage lettuces cut, and a handful of sorrel, four carrots, and four turnips. Fry them all together, taking care not to burn them. Take a piece of butter and put it into the stew pan. Melt it, and when it has turned brown, put in by degrees as much flour as will thicken the soup. Stir it well, and add it to the first mentioned gravy stock. Before it boils, put in the fried vegetables and stew them very gently. If in season, throw in a pint of green pease, and stew all together until tender. Season well. The soup would be as thick as good cream.'

VEGETABLES

To Stew Red Cabbage

This recipe comes from Ann Peckham's book, published in 1767.

'Take your cabbage and cut it fine, leaving out the large veins, boil it till tender, and drain it; then put it into a sauce-pan with a little melted butter, two spoonfuls of vinegar, a little pepper and salt, two spoonfuls of gravy, keep it stirring over your stove six minutes, then serve it up hot with fryed saucesages round it.'

Bubble and Squeak

This old recipe follows the traditional formula, used since the sixteenth century. It was only during the Victorian era that boiled potatoes were added to the dish. This recipe comes from Ann Peckham's book, published in 1767.

'Take cabbage, boil and drain it, cut it small, and put it into a stew-pan with butter, and some young onions cut small; take some slices of beef that hath been either boiled or roasted, fry them, and put to them a little vinegar, pepper, salt and a spoonful of gravy. Serve it up hot.'

Stuffed Mushrooms

12 large flat mushrooms
some small mushrooms
1 medium onion
3 egg yolks
Yorkshire relish
parsley
thyme
seasoning
butter

Chop the small mushrooms and the stalks from the large ones. Mix with the herbs and onion, all finely chopped. Melt some butter and when hot but not brown, fry the mushroom mixture. Blend in the relish and the egg yolks, stir well and cook for a few minutes. Butter an oven dish and place the flat mushrooms in it. Top each one with some of the fried mixture and bake in a moderate oven for 15 minutes.

serves 3.

Baked Onions

4 large onions
1 rasher bacon
1 carrot
good stock
2 cloves
1 bay leaf
thyme, chopped
parsley, chopped
a pinch of ground mace
seasoning
butter

Peel the onions and put into an oven dish. Pour in the stock to come about 2½ cm (an inch) up the sides. Add a little chopped thyme and parsley, the mace, cloves and a bay leaf broken into pieces. Peel and chop the carrot and add to the dish with the diced rasher of bacon. Season, cover and bake in a moderate oven until almost tender. This will take approximately 3 hours. Remove the lid and bake uncovered for a further 30 minutes. Put a large knob of butter on each onion before serving.

serves 4.

Parsnip Fritters

2 parsnips
25g (1 oz) butter
2 tablespoons flour

Prepare the parsnips and cook until tender, then mash them until they are quite smooth. Season well and beat in 25g (1 ounce) or more of butter. Stir in the flour, just enough to make the mixture moderately firm. Have some hot fat ready in a frying pan and fry the parsnip mixture in spoonfuls. Serve hot with fried bacon.

serves 3.

Spinach with Poached Eggs

This an old Yorkshire recipe of 1769.

'Take two or three handfuls of young spinach, pick it from the stalks, wash and drain it very clean, put it into a pan with a lump of butter and a little salt, and keep stirring it all the time till it be done enough, then take it out and squeeze out the water. Chop it and add a little more butter, lay it in your dish in quarters, and betwixt every quarter a poached egg, and one in the middle. Fry some sippets of white bread and put them into your spinach, so serve it up.'

To Stew Pease

1 litre (1 quart) peas
2 goss (cos) lettuces
4 onions
salt and pepper
gravy
225g (½ lb) butter
flour

This recipe comes from Ann Peckham's book, published in 1767. This delicious dish can be reduced in quantity and used easily in present-day kitchens.

'Take a stew pan, and butter the inside well, then put in a quart of pease, two goss lettuce cut small, four onions, some pepper and salt to your taste, cover the pan close, and let them stew ten minutes, then put in gravy to moisten the whole, let them stew gently a quarter of an hour shaking the pan, put in half a pound of butter at different times, adding a little flour to thicken, when near enough, take it to the onions, and serve hot.'

Vegetable Roll

suetcrust pastry
2 medium sized potatoes
2 small carrots *or* 1 large
2 small tomatoes
1 parsnip
½ small turnip
1 level dessertspoon
   Marmite
seasoning

Roll out the pastry fairly thinly and smear with the Marmite. Prepare the vegetables—slice the potatoes very thinly and grate the others. Place over the pastry and cover with the sliced tomatoes. Season well and roll up. Place in a cloth and steam for 2½ hours.

SALADS

Pig's Trotter Salad

4 pig's trotters
2 medium carrots
1 medium onion
100g (4 oz) shredded onion
175g (6 oz) diced tomato
150ml (¼ pint) French
  dressing
2 tablespoons chopped parsley
seasoning

This is a recipe from The Black Swan Hotel, Helmsley.

Simmer the trotters in salt water with the prepared and chopped onion and carrots for approximately 2½ hours. After this time the meat should come away from the bone easily. If not, keep simmering until it will. Remove the trotters from the stock and take all the meat and flesh from the bones. Place the meat in a basin, press and refrigerate overnight. Turn the meat out of the basin and cut into long, thin strips, mix well with the French dressing, tomato, shredded onion and chopped parsley, and season to taste.

Dress in an hors d'oeuvre dish and sprinkle with chopped parsley.

serves 6.

To Make Solomongundy

This is a recipe taken from Ann Peckham's book published in Leeds in 1767 and inscribed 'Well known to have been for Forty Years one of the most noted cooks in the county of York.'

'Mince very fine some white of chicken, or veal, and the yolks of hard eggs all separate, a little hang beef or tongue, and some pickled cucumber shred fine, some parsley and shallot shred; take a china dish that you intend to lay it on, lay a deep plate on your dish the wrong side upwards. You may lay it in what form you like, as a star, a pyramid, or in squares, and you may lay it round capers, anchovy, lemon and barberries.'

Salamongundy

This is Hannah Glasse's recipe of 1747.

'Take two or three Roman or Cabbage Lettuces, and when you have washed them clean, swing them pretty dry in a cloth; then beginning at the open end, cut them cross-ways, as fine as a good big thread, and lay the lettuces so cut, about an inch thick, all over the bottom of a dish. When you have thus garnished your dish, take two cold roasted pullets or chickens, and cut the flesh off the breasts and wings into slices, about three inches long, a quarter of an inch broad, and as thin as a shilling; lay them upon the lettuce round the end to the middle of the dish, and the other towards the brim; then having boned and cut six anchovies, each into eight pieces, lay them all between each slice of the fowls, then cut the lean meat off the legs into dice, and cut a lemon into small dice; then mince the yolks of four eggs, three or four anchovies, and a little parsley, and make a round heap of these in your dish, piling it up in the form of a sugar-loaf, and garnish it with onions, as big as the yolks of eggs, boiled in a good deal of water very tender and white. Put the largest of the onions in the middle on the top of the Salamongundy, and lay the rest all round the brim of the dish, as thick as you can lay them; then beat some sallad oil up with vinegar, salt and papper, and pour over it all. Garnish with grapes just scalded, or french beans blanched, or Stertion-flowers, and serve it up for a first course.'

Chicken Salad

This simple recipe was given to me by an elderly housewife living in Swaledale. She explained that she always used home-made mayonnaise in the salad.

'Cut up the flesh from a good-sized, cooked chicken and put in a bowl with a shredded, crisp lettuce. Add as much celery as liked, about half a medium-sized one cut into small pieces. Pour on some creamy mayonnaise and stir lightly together. Line a bowl with lettuce leaves and put the chicken salad in the centre. Quarter some hard-boiled eggs and garnish the salad with them.'

This is slightly reminiscent of the early recipes for Solomongundy or Salamagundy (see above), the shredded lettuce and celery being mentioned by Eliza Acton in her notes on the preparation of salads: 'They are better when not prepared until near the time of sending them to table and should not be sauced until the instant before they are served.—In England it is customary to cut the lettuces extremely fine; the French, who object to the flavour of the knife, which they fancy this mode imparts, break them small instead. Young celery alone, sliced and dressed with a rich salad mixture is excellent; it is still in some families, served thus always with roast pheasant.'

Beetroot Salad

boiled beetroot
1 bought lemon jelly
425ml (¾ pint) water
2 tablespoons vinegar
a little grated onion
salt

Prepare the lemon jelly as directed on the packet but use only 425ml (three-quarters of a pint) of water minus two tablespoons. To the jelly add the vinegar, salt and a little grated onion. When the jelly is almost set stir in as much boiled, chopped beetroot as liked.

Mrs Gott's Spring Salad

1 large onion or a large bunch of chives
1 large crisp lettuce
a bunch of mint
2 tablespoons sugar
vinegar

Chop the onion, lettuce and mint. Mix with the sugar and put into a glass bowl. Cover with vinegar and garnish with a sprig of mint. Use for all cold meats.

Mrs Gott also recommends adding tiny cooked new potatoes to the dish.

SAVOURIES

Yorkshire Pudding

75g + 1 dessertspoon (3 oz) plain flour
275ml (½ pint) milk
1 egg
a scant half-teaspoon of salt

There are as many recipes for Yorkshire pudding, all claiming to be the best, as days in a week, so I give the one I was given by an elderly Yorkshire woman some years ago and which I have always found successful. On occasion I have varied it slightly according to some newly garnered information. I have left it to stand for some hours or cooked it immediately; added a handful of freshly fallen soft snow and beaten it beside an open window- even outdoors. None of these appeared to alter the end product to any noticeable degree.

Whisk the egg well, add a little of the milk and work in the flour and salt gradually. Beat well with a fork or holed straining spoon. Add the remaining milk and use when required. Heat some dripping in a baking tin until hot, pour in the batter and cook until well risen at 230°C (450°F), Gas Mark 8, about 20 minutes.

The recipe for this pudding appeared in a book published in 1737, *The Whole Duty of Woman*, where it was suggested to make use of the juices and fats which dripped from the joint roasting on the spit.

serves 6.

Hannah Glasse's Yorkshire Pudding

Here is Hannah Glasse's recipe, which appeared in 1747, being the first time this recipe was called Yorkshire Pudding.

'Take a Quart of Milk, four Eggs, and a little Salt, make it up into a thick Batter with Flour, like a Pancake Batter. You must have a good Piece of Meat at the Fire, take a Stew-pan end put some Dripping in, set it on the Fire; when it boils, pour in your Pudding; let it bake on the Fire till you think it is nigh enough, then turn a Plate upside-down in the Dripping-pan, that the Dripping may not be blacked; set your Stew-pan on it under your Meat, and let the Dripping drop on the Pudding and the Heat of the Fire come to it, to make it of a fine Brown. When your Meat is done and sent to Table, drain all the Fat from your Pudding, and set it on the Fire again to dry a little; then slide it as dry as you can into a Dish, melt some Butter, and pour it into a Cup, and set it in the middle of the Pudding. It is an exceeding good Pudding; the Gravy of the Meat eats well with it.'

Yorkshire Savoury Pudding

275ml (½ pint) boiling milk
   or water
225g (½ lb) breadcrumbs
25g (1 oz) oatmeal
100g (4 oz) shredded suet
4 large onions
1 – 2 teaspoons sage
seasoning

Numerous recipes for two basic types of savoury or herb puddings have survived in Yorkshire. The first is one which consisted mainly of breadcrumbs, onions, oatmeal and sage.

Pour boiling milk or water over the breadcrumbs and leave for 30 minutes. Stir and mix with the oatmeal. Chop the sage and onions, and mix into the breadcrumbs with the suet. Season well and put into a well-buttered oven dish. Bake until brown at 190°C (375°F), Gas Mark 5, for approximately 40 minutes. Slice and serve with beef and thick gravy.

serves 6.

To Make a Herb Pudding

The second basic type of savoury pudding from Ann Peckham's recipe, 1767, used a wide variety of plants such as sorrel, thyme, spinach, parsley and marigold flowers. Elizabeth Raffald's recipe from her book of 1796 (*The Experienced English Housekeeper*) also included beets and leeks. Jane Lister in her book published in

Leeds in 1741 used currants, eggs, cream and oatmeal together with wild herbs and plants.

'Take a good quantity of parsley and spinage, a little thyme and marrygold flowers, put to them a gill of creed oat-meal, shred them very small with a little beef suet, a few crumbs of bread, a gill of cream, four eggs, and a little salt, mix all very well together, dredge your cloth and tie it close, it will take a good deal of boiling.'

Black Pudding

Black puddings are usually heated in water and served with mustard. Bread and butter or boiled potatoes are familiar accompaniments but often the puddings are sliced and grilled to serve with bacon. Methods of making vary according to local taste and it is possible to buy them in Yorkshire 'with or without fat'. Those containing fat are more popular. Most black pudding makers include certain 'secret' ingredients which they refuse to reveal but old recipes usually contain a number of herbs such as thyme, winter savory or pennyroyal. Sage and mint were also used with barley, oatmeal and the blood.

The following is an eighteenth-century recipe originally called Hog's Pudding.

'Take a quantity of groats or rough oatmeal. Scald with boiling milk or water. Cover with a cloth and leave to swell all night. Next morning pour off the thin part of the collected blood into which had been put some pennyroyal. Pour the thick blood on to the oatmeal—enough to make it black. Add pepper and salt, and a little shredded part of the green of a leek. Add some fat or flead of a pig, cut finely, or beef suet, and one or two eggs. Put into pie dishes or a dripping tin and bake about an hour, or put into your prepared skins and boil them.'

Savoury Ducks

225g (½ lb) finely chopped pig's liver
225g (½ lb) finely chopped beef suet

Savoury ducks (or faggots) and harslet are still made in many butchers' shops in Yorkshire from ingredients similar to those traditionally used – the liver, lights, heart and sweetbread from the pig, but any oddments left after pig-killing were often

225g (½ lb) finely chopped
  onions
225g (½ lb) breadcrumbs
pig's flead
2 small eggs
1 tablespoon fresh sage
cayenne
salt and pepper

included; now it is more usual for the butcher just to use the pig's liver, raw pork and sometimes the heart. Both are seasoned with herbs, and oatmeal or breadcrumbs added. Faggots are customarily shaped into small domed portions, each one wrapped in a portion of the flead and baked. Harslet is more usually cooked as a large globe-shape, again wrapped in the flead and baked or roasted. This recipe from a book dated 1843 includes only the pig's liver.

Beat the eggs and mix all the ingredients well together. Shape into balls and wrap each one in a piece of the pig's flead. Put into a greased tin and bake in a hot oven until brown. Eat with a little gravy poured over.

serves 6.

Pease Pudding

225g (8 oz) split peas
25g (1 oz) butter
1 egg, beaten
1 ham bone or bacon scraps
seasoning

Wash the peas and soak overnight in cold water. Tie the peas loosely in a cloth and put in a saucepan of boiling water to cover, with a pinch of salt and the ham bone or bacon scraps. Boil the peas for 2-2½ hours, or until soft. Take out the bag, sieve the peas and add the butter, egg and seasoning. This should be beaten until thoroughly mixed and then tightly tied in a floured cloth and boiled for another ½ hour.

This is usually served with boiled ham or bacon.

serves 4.

Stilton, Celery and Walnut Fritters

100g (4 oz) Stilton cheese
1 large stick celery, finely
  chopped
15g (½ oz) walnuts, finely
  chopped
1 egg

This recipe comes from The Black Swan Hotel, Helmsley.

Grate the cheese, or pass through a sieve to purée. Add the finely chopped celery and walnuts. Beat the egg and use enough to moisten to a suitable consistency for rolling. Check for seasoning – freshly ground black pepper is a good addition, also a pinch of herbs or fresh chopped parsley. Shape into small balls,

seasoning
herbs
flour
egg
breadcrumbs

dip in flour, egg and breadcrumbs, and deep fry for 3 or 4 minutes until golden brown. Serve with a bowl of tomato pickle or chutney.

serves 2.

Wensleydale Eggs

4 eggs
75g (3 oz) cheese
50g (2 oz) grated cheese
3 tablespoons cream
breadcrumbs
butter

Slice the cheese thinly and place in a greased baking dish. Break in the eggs and add seasoning. Pour on the cream and cover with breadcrumbs and grated cheese. Dot with butter and bake in a hot oven for 15 minutes.

serves 4.

To Make Eggs in Moonshine

eggs
oil
salt
1 onion
dry cider
grated nutmeg

This is one of Ann Peckham's recipes, 1767.

'Break your eggs into a dish upon some oil either melted or cold, strew some salt on them, and set them over a chaffing-dish of coals, and cover them; but make not the yolks too hard; make your sauce of an onion cut in round slices, and fried in good oil; put to them a little verjuice [dry cider], salt and grated nutmeg, and serve them up hot.'

Bacon and Egg Pie

225g (½ lb) shortcrust pastry
2 rashers streaky bacon
2 eggs
150ml (¼ pint) milk (approx.)
1 teaspoon parsley
salt and pepper

This recipe is taken from the Yorkshire Woman's Institute book,
Line a 20-cm (eight-inch) baking tin with the shortcrust pastry, rolled fairly thin. Cut up the bacon into small pieces and put on to the pastry. Beat the eggs and add enough milk to make 275ml (half a pint) of liquid. Season, stir well, and pour over bacon in the pastry. Sprinkle with the pastry. Put on to the middle shelf of the oven and bake until set and browned at 230°C (450°F), Gas Mark 8.
The above pie may also be made with pastry lid brushed over with beaten egg before putting it in the oven. Bake in the hottest part of the oven for a few minutes and then lower the heat until the pie is cooked.

serves 6.

Cheese Pudding

225g (½ lb) cheese
575ml (1 pint) milk
2 eggs
50g (2 oz) butter
175g (6 oz) breadcrumbs
a little grated onion
seasoning

Warm the milk and pour on to the breadcrumbs. Beat in the butter, eggs, onion and seasoning. Grate the cheese, keep 50g (two ounces) for topping and add the remainder to the mixture, beating well. Put into a buttered oven dish, sprinkle with remaining cheese and bake in a moderate oven, 180°C (350°F) Gas Mark 4, for 45 minutes.

This is delicious as a high tea dish.

serves 4

Swaledale Pie

450g (1 lb) cooked chicken,
    meat, *or* fish
675g (½ lb) cooked,
    mashed potato
100g (4 oz) lightly cooked
    mushrooms
boiled onions and a little of the
    water in which they were
    cooked
seasoning
cayenne pepper (optional)

A dish which makes good use of any cooked, left-over meat, fish or poultry.

Butter an oven dish and line with potato, keeping some for a topping. Chop the onions and put into the dish with the selected meat. Season well, adding a dash of cayenne pepper if liked. Put in the mushrooms and a little of the onion water. Cover with the remaining potato and bake in a moderate oven until brown.

serves 6.

Puddings

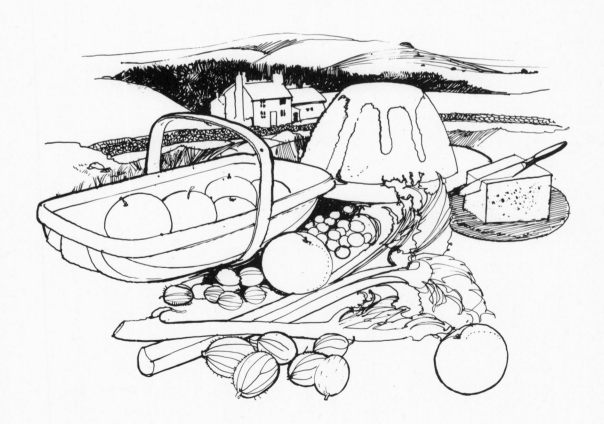

Puddings

We have in this country been noted for the excellence of our puddings for many years. Misson wrote his famous book in 1719 (*M. Misson's Memoirs*: *Observations on his travels over England*) describing English cookery and extolling the puddings of the land where: 'They bake them in an oven, they boil them with meat, they make them fifty several ways: BLESSED BE HE THAT INVENTED PUDDING, for it is manna that hits the palates of all sorts of people.' Certainly in Yorkshire a home-made pudding of fine quality has always rounded off a good dinner to perfection.

Until Victorian times the robust steamed or boiled puddings popular with cottagers were not esteemed highly in aristocratic circles where creams, custards and a wealth of 'conceits' bedecked the table. In humble homes the boiled pudding, perhaps cooked to serve with bacon, might be sliced and served after the meal with stewed fruit or simply sugared and presented with a dish of thick cream from the dairy. I know of some families where until twenty or thirty years ago Yorkshire pudding was regularly served like this. Boiling was often the only method of cooking puddings in homes without ovens and the popularity of suet puddings dates from this period.

When the Corn Laws were repealed the village of Pudsey celebrated the event by making an enormous pudding of flour, suet, fruit and other ingredients. Twenty women each mixed a separate portion then the whole mixture was blended and steamed in a dye-pan at a local mill. A windlass was used to lift the pudding into the pan where it was cooked for three days and nights. The ingredients weighed a total of twenty stones and, when cooked, the pudding was wheeled through the streets in procession to the field where it was to be served. People came from miles around to share in the celebration, everyone bringing their own plate and cutlery.

With the Victorian era steamed puddings became fashionable, but too often middle-class families ruined the reputation of English cooking by seeking to follow fashion at the cost of quality. Variety became all-important, with consequent waste in the kitchen, and the mistress of the house pared expenses by insisting that the cook used less costly substitutes. Cornflour replaced eggs, cheaper fats were used instead of butter and cream became an item of luxury. Delicious suet puddings, filled with fresh gooseberries and lightly scented with elderflowers or with apples having an elusive flavour of quince, presented in steaming succulence with a jug of thick cream, have been insidiously replaced by packages offering 'instant' sweet delights.

Rice puddings made with butter, brown sugar, and spices or vanilla pods and served with thick cream have gradually since the eighteenth century degenerated from a creamy golden enticing dish, once highly regarded, to a thin tasteless gruel I should hesitate to give to my dog. An eighteenth-century recipe for rice pudding used cream instead of milk, sugar, rice, lemon peel, nutmeg and eggs for the richly pleasing dish then popular. (See page 95 for a modern recipe.)

Accustomed to feeding appreciative families of good appetite, and inheritors of the belief that home-made is best, Yorkshire women excel in home-baking and not least in the quality of their puddings. A much-quoted Yorkshire saying 'An apple pie without some cheese is like a kiss without a squeeze' refers to a favourite type of pudding in the county. Fruit pies have figured largely upon tea and dinner tables since the earliest ovens were built into Yorkshire homes. Gooseberries and rhubarb are greatly esteemed and are made into pies and puddings of all kinds—sponge, suet, crumbles, cobblers or fools. An eighteenth-century writer referring to Leeds wrote that after the open-air cloth market had finished on the two days it was held each week, other traders moved in and 'Fruit of all sortes are brought in so vast quantities, that Halifax, and other considerable markets, are frequently supplied from hence, the mayors officers have number'd five hundred loads of apples only, upon one day.'

Steamed puddings, bringing nostalgic smiles to the lips of most men, are served splendidly in Yorkshire where fresh fruit and cream are used abundantly. (See page 97.) Bread-and-butter puddings to delight the palate are created lovingly and left to stand for hours before cooking so that the spices, eggs, butter, bread and creamy milk amalgamate to form a light pudding of regal perfection.

Most Yorkshire housewives will admit that although a suet pudding can be made in minutes, long slow cooking is essential if a light and airy result is desired; similarly with many puddings. A bilberry tart takes no longer to prepare to cook than a packed 'instant' dessert, and many families enjoy expending a little time and energy on gathering the fruit themselves from some nearby moorland. Bilberries are also readily available in Yorkshire markets in season so it is possible, despite the limitations on time imposed by work outside the home, to make puddings that follow the traditional pattern of Yorkshire cooking. (See page 101 for a delicious recipe.) Quickly mixed steamed puddings are made at weekends when it is possible to fit in other chores while occasionally checking the water level so that the pudding does not boil dry nor the water go off the boil, since this would cause a lessening of lightness—the quality so greatly desired in a steamed pudding. No northern housewife worth her salt would be satisfied with anything less than a pudding 'light as love'.

Frumenty 1

Possibly the oldest English dish still being made in rural areas is frumenty, which is made of hulled or pearled wheat boiled until soft, then, in its thick, gelatinous form, cooked with milk, fruit and spices as a festive dish, or eaten simply with milk and honey at breakfast-time. In some parts of the north-east of Yorkshire it was traditionally served on Christmas morning; Whitby and Filey celebrated Christmas Eve with dishes of frumenty followed by apple pie and cheese or gingerbread and I have been told of families in the Pennine Dales where it is still a customary Christmas Eve dish. The rich festive version has been described as the nearest dish one could imagine to a liquid spice loaf, and a fourteenth-century version included saffron, egg yolks and 'cowe mylk'.

Cree the wheat by cooking it in water slowly for 12 hours; this can be done near a fire left in all night. Use 450g (a pound) of wheat for six to eight servings. Strain off any surplus water and boil the wheat until thick and sticky. This is now ready for serving with milk, spices and sugar as a breakfast dish, or it can be cooked in 1 litre (two pints) of milk with dried fruit, spices and sugar until hot. It can also be thickened with a paste of flour and cold milk or egg yolks and this rich version is customarily served with a nut of butter in each dish and perhaps a splash of rum.

One Yorkshire version of 1826 suggests 'Serve in soup plates, putting in a piece of butter before serving, and – for adults – flavour with whisky. A favourite Christmas Eve dish.'

Frumenty 2

225g (½ lb) pearled wheat
575ml (1 pint) milk
25g (1 oz) sugar
mixed spice and cinnamon to
    taste
dried fruit if liked

Cree the wheat by covering with water. Bring to the boil, then leave for 12 hours (overnight is ideal) in a warm place such as beside an open fire or on a warm radiator. Drain off surplus water and simmer the wheat until soft, stirring often.

Pour in the milk, add the sugar, spices and dried fruit and cook until thick. Serve at breakfast-time or, as is still traditional in parts of Yorkshire, on Christmas Eve.

Albert Pudding

100g + 2 dessertspoons (4 oz)
    flour
75g (3 oz) sugar
100g (4 oz) butter
2 large eggs, beaten
100g (4 oz) raisins
grated lemon rind

For the sauce:
75g (3 oz) butter
50g (2 oz) sugar
2 teaspoons brandy
2 teaspoons lemon juice

This is one of a range of puddings which became popular during the Victorian era, most likely because of the Germanic influence of the Prince Consort. May Byron gives a Yorkshire origin to the pudding in her book *Pot-Luck* but it is a type that was widespread in the period when Royal Coburg Pudding and Kassel Pudding were among other pudding recipes with German names in Victorian cookery books.

Beat the butter until pale and gradually add the beaten eggs. Continue to beat until fluffy then fold in the flour. Add the sugar and grated lemon rind. Mix well, then stir in the raisins and put into a buttered basin. Cover well and steam for 3 hours.

For the sauce. Melt the butter, stir in the sugar, lemon juice and brandy and serve hot, poured over the pudding.

serves 6.

Clapham Pudding

100g + 2 dessertspoons (4 oz)
    plain flour
100g + 2 dessertspoons (4 oz)
    ground rice
100g + 1 dessertspoon (4 oz)
    suet
100g + 1 dessertspoon (4 oz)
    sugar
150ml (¼ pint) milk
100g (4 oz) sultanas
1 small teaspoonful bicarbonate
    of soda
a pinch of salt

Put the sultanas, flour, sugar, salt, ground rice and suet into a bowl. Warm the milk and dissolve in it the bicarbonate of soda. Pour on to the dry ingredients and mix thoroughly. Pour the mixture into a buttered basin, cover and steam for 3 hours. Serve with fresh cream or thick custard sauce.

serves 6.

Marmalade Pudding

100g + 4 dessertspoons (4 oz)
    fresh breadcrumbs
100g + 1 dessertspoon (4 oz)
    shredded suet
100g + 1 dessertspoon (4 oz)
    soft brown sugar
2 eggs
2 tablespoons marmalade
a pinch of salt

Beat the eggs and mix all the ingredients together. Put into a buttered basin and leave at least 1 hour to stand before cooking, or overnight if possible. Cover securely and steam for 2½ to 3 hours. Serve with a hot sauce or custard.

serves 6.

Lemon Pudding

50g + 1 dessertspoon (2 oz)
  plain flour
50g + 2 dessertspoons (2 oz)
  fresh breadcrumbs
100g + 1 dessertspoon (4 oz)
  shredded suet
50g + ½ dessertspoon (2 oz)
  sugar
2 tablespoons golden
  syrup
1 egg
½ teacupful milk
1 lemon
a pinch of salt

Grate the lemon rind and mix into the flour, breadcrumbs, and suet. Beat the eggs and add to the dry ingredients with the lemon juice, syrup, sugar and finally milk. Beat the mixture together thoroughly and put into a buttered basin. Steam for 2 hours and then turn out. This pudding looks most appetizing presented in a shallow bowl, decorated with twists of lemon slices and surrounded by a steaming hot, tangy lemon sauce (see below).

serves 6.

Lemon Sauce

1 large lemon
25g (1 oz) butter
2 tablespoons flour
1½ tablespoons sugar
1 *or* 2 egg yolks
150ml (¼ pint) water

Grate the rind into the sugar. Melt the butter in a pan, stir in the flour gradually, then add the water a little at a time and stir continuously until the mixture comes to the boil. Simmer slowly for 2 or 3 minutes. Add the sugar and lemon juice. Remove from the heat and stir in the yolks.

Masters Sunday Pudding

225g (½ lb) plain flour
150g + 3 dessertspoons (6 oz)
  shredded suet
25g (1 oz) Demerara sugar
3 tablespoons golden syrup
2 eggs
225g (½ lb) sultanas
1 teaspoon bicarbonate of soda
milk
a pinch of salt

This recipe comes from Mrs Bryant, a young housewife living in the York area. Her family particularly enjoy her version of this pudding, which she describes as a kind of everyday Christmas Pudding.

Beat the eggs thoroughly. Stir together the flour, suet, sugar, salt and sultanas. Warm the syrup and add with the eggs. Mix the bicarbonate of soda with a little milk and beat into the mixture, adding more milk if necessary to give a soft mixture. Butter a basin, put in the mixture and cover well. Steam for about 4 hours and serve with custard.

serves 6.

Queer Times Pudding

1 cup breadcrumbs
1 cup flour
50g (2 oz) suet
1 cup sugar
1 cup currants
2 teaspoons baking powder
a pinch of salt
milk

Mix all the ingredients well with a little milk. Put into a greased basin, cover and steam for 2 hours. Serve with custard sauce.

serves 4.

Rice Pudding

40g (1½ oz) shortgrain rice
575ml (1 pint milk) *or*
   425ml (¾ pint) milk and
   150ml (¼ pint) single cream
40 – 50g (1½ – 2 oz) Demerara
   sugar
40g (1½ oz) butter
ground nutmeg
1 vanilla pod (optional)

Wash the rice well in cold water. Put it into a basin with the sugar and butter. If a vanilla pod is used put it with the milk into a saucepan and simmer gently for five minutes then leave to infuse a further fifteen. Pour into the basin with the cream, removing the vanilla pod. If this vanilla flavouring is not wanted, heat the milk and pour into the basin with the cream. Stir, sprinkle the top of the milk with ground nutmeg and cook until the rice is tender. This will take about two hours at 160°C (325°F), Gas Mark 3.

serves 4.

Brown Betty

2 dozen large apples
1 loaf stale bread
brown sugar
butter
spice of preference

This is an old Yorkshire recipe.

'Take two dozen fine large apples, and cut them into thin slices, pare them if preferred; crumb up a loaf of stale bread. Take a deep pudding-dish, put in a layer of bread crumbs, then one of apples, sprinkle over them some brown sugar, put in a piece of butter and any spice that may be preferred, then sprinkle in a very little cold water. Put in another layer of crumbs, apples, sugar, butter, spice, and water again; go on until the dish is full, making the top layer of apples. Bake in a quick oven. Eat hot sprinkled with sugar and a wine sauce, or fresh cream.'

serves 20.

Rich Wine Sauce

6 egg yolks
50 g (2 oz) sugar
7 tablespoons sherry

Put all the ingredients into a basin over a pan of hot water and whisk until the sauce thickens. Serve at once.

Wakefield Pudding

450g (1 lb) apples
50g (2 oz) sugar
425ml (¾ pint) water
stale bread

Peel, core and cut up the apples. Stew them in the water with the sugar until soft. Line a buttered basin with some of the bread and put some apple on the bottom, then alternate layers of bread and fruit until the basin is full. The top layer must be bread. Put a plate on top which just fits inside the basin rim. Place a weight on it and leave in a cold place overnight. Turn out, sprinkle with sugar and serve with cream.

serves 6.

White Pot

3 slices white bread
225g (½ lb) apples
50g (2 oz) suet
50g (2 oz) currants
25g (1 oz) raisins
75g (3 oz) sugar
¼ – ½ teaspoon ground
   nutmeg
4 eggs
575ml (1 pint) milk

Place a layer of white bread cut thin on the bottom of an oven dish, then a layer of apples cut thin, then a layer of suet, currants, raisins, sugar and nutmeg; then another layer of bread, and so on, as above, till the dish is filled up. Beat four eggs, and mix them with 575ml (a pint) of good milk, a little sugar and nutmeg, and pour it over the top. This should be made 3 or 4 hours before it is baked for 45 minutes at 190°C (375°F), Gas Mark 5.

serves 6.

Fruity Roly-Poly

450g (1 lb) baking apples
225g (½ lb) suetcrust pastry
75g (3 oz) Demerara sugar
75g (3 oz) raisins
ground nutmeg

Peel and slice the apples thinly. Roll the pastry into a oblong 1¼cm (half an inch) thick. Place the apples down the centre and cover with the sugar. Sprinkle on the raisins and a little nutmeg. Dampen the edges and roll, sealing the ends well. Wrap in greaseproof paper then in a floured cloth. Secure tightly but leave room to expand. Steam for 2½ hours and serve with custard or a sweet sauce.

serves 6.

Scarborough Pudding

225g (½ lb) red plums
75g (3 oz) tapioca
75g (3 oz) sugar
575ml (1 pint) water

Wash and drain the tapioca. Put into a buttered pie-dish with the sugar and water. Halve the plums, stone them and mix in the other ingredients. Cook in a moderate oven for 1 hour and serve with cream.

serves 4.

Ilkley Pudding

450g (1 lb) raspberries
225g (½ lb) red currants
225g (½ lb) sugar
thin well buttered slices of
    bread

Stew the fruit in a little water, then sieve and add the sugar. Line a pudding basin with thin buttered bread. Warm the fruit purée and fill the basin with alternate layers of fruit and buttered bread, ending with the latter. Put a plate on the top, with a heavy weight upon it. Leave to stand all night, then turn out and serve with a good custard or cream.

This pudding can be made with bilberries, or blackberry and apple, etc.

serves 6.

Rhubarb Cobbler

450g (1 lb) rhubarb
150g + 3 dessertspoons (6 oz)
    self-raising flour
25g (1 oz) margarine
5 dessertspoons sugar
milk
sugar to taste
a pinch of salt

Rub the margarine into the sieved flour and salt, add sugar and mix to a scone-like consistency with milk. Roll out and cut into rounds or squares depending on shape of dish. Cut rhubarb into neat pieces and cook for 10 minutes with 2 – 3 tablespoons water and sugar to taste. Arrange the scone dough on top of the rhubarb in a fireproof dish and cook for about 15 minutes in a fairly hot oven.

serves 6.

A Delicate Fig Pudding

This is an old Yorkshire recipe.

'For a delicate fig pudding, choose good pulled figs, soak overnight in enough claret to cover them; in the morn simmer gently in the oven with claret to replace that absorbed by the figs. Sweeten slightly. Cook until the skins are tender then set to cool. Serve covered with whipped cream both sweetened and flavoured with sherry.'

An adaptation of this rather rich dish is much liked in rural areas where figs are lightly stewed with sugar to taste, and a good scattering of elderflowers, which impart a delicate and delicious flavour. This dish is also served chilled and with fresh cream.

Baked Stuffed Apples

Wash and core as many large baking apples as required. Prick each one a few times with a fork to prevent bursting and put into an oven dish with a little water. Fill the centres with mincemeat and bake in a moderate oven until the apples are tender. This will take about 45 minutes. A little home-made sweet wine or a teaspoonful of brandy can be poured on to the mincemeat before serving with thick fresh cream.

A mixture of dried fruits or sultanas and dates can be used instead of mincemeat. Mix with brown sugar and the juice and grated rind of a lemon before using.

Codling Cream

baking apples
white wine
575ml (1 pint) cream
2 egg yolks
rose water (from
　chemists)
sugar

This recipe is taken from a collection of manuscript recipes, circa 1800, from the Blanch Leigh Collection, Leeds University.

'Take codlings [baking apples] and boil 'em in white wine till ye are soft, drain all ye liquor from 'em and strain ye pulph thro' a strainer, take 1 pint of cream and boil it and thicken it with ye yolkes of 2 eggs and while its hot put in ye pulph wch must be season'd wth rose-water and sugr.'

Tipsy Cake

1 large stale sponge cake
575ml (1 pint) thick, rich
　custard
275ml (½ pint) fresh, double
　cream
1 small glass brandy
sufficient sherry to soak
　the cake
apricot jam
blanched or lightly roasted
　almonds (optional)
glacé cherries (optional)
strips of angelica (optional)

Split the cake and spread with a good layer of jam. Put the two halves together in a glass dish and carefully pour over the sherry and brandy. Leave to soak for about 1 hour, then cover with the cooled custard. Decorate lavishly with thick cream, and garnish with the cherries and angelica or with the almonds cut into long splinters and stuck all over.

Tipsy Cake is more typical if the cake has been baked in a basin, but it must then be split into extra layers to be spread with jam for the traditional domed effect.

Gooseberry Fool

675g (1½ lb) gooseberries
100g (4 oz) sugar
275ml (½ pint) double cream,
　lightly whipped
2 tablespoons water

Prepare the gooseberries and place in a pan with the water. Cook gently, stirring frequently until the gooseberries are soft. Sieve, reserving a few for decoration, and stir in the sugar. When cold stir in the lightly whipped cream and pour into a dish. Decorate with the whole fruits and serve chilled.

serves 6.

Rhubarb Tansy

450g (1 lb) rhubarb
100g (4 oz) sugar
100g (4 oz) butter
2 egg yolks
150ml (¼ pint) double cream
2 tablespoons lemon juice

This dish was traditionally made with the juice of the tansy, now replaced by lemon juice.

Prepare the rhubarb and cut into 2½ cm (1-inch) lengths. Melt the butter, add the rhubarb pieces and simmer very gently until tender. Stir in the sugar and allow to dissolve. Whip the egg yolks and cream together lightly and add to the rhubarb. Stir over a very low heat until thick but do not overheat. Pour into a dish to serve hot or cold, sprinkled with the lemon juice.

serves 6.

Flannel Cakes

225g (½ lb) flour
25g (1 oz) castor sugar
25g (1 oz) butter
2 eggs
425ml (¾ pint) of milk
½ level teaspoon bicarbonate
   of soda
a pinch of salt

Sift together the flour, bicarbonate of soda and salt and rub in the butter. Add the sugar and egg yolks. Gradually blend in the milk. Whisk the egg whites until stiff and fold in. Lightly grease a frying pan and when fairly hot pour in enough batter to form a thin pancake. When the surface bubbles, turn to cook the other side.

Pile the cakes on a dish and keep them warm, and serve as soon as possible with strawberry jam, warmed and slightly diluted.

makes 12.

Shrovetide Fritters

450g (1 lb) flour
100g + 1 dessertspoon (4 oz)
   sugar
50g + ½ dessertspoon (2 oz)
   lard
4 eggs
100g (4 oz) currants
25g (1 oz) fresh yeast
a pinch each of salt, mixed
   spice and ground nutmeg
milk to mix

These fritters were made every year in many parts of England on Collop Monday, the day before Shrove Tuesday. In Yorkshire it was the custom for children to go out 'colloping' on this day when they would beg:

Pray, dame, a collop,
Or we'll give you a wallop.

Some small gift was usually forthcoming, originally a collop of bacon or fat in which to cook the pancakes on Shrove Tuesday.

Rub the lard into the flour then add the salt and spices. Stir in the fruit and sugar. Beat the eggs and add with the yeast. Beat very thoroughly and mix to a thick batter with milk. Leave to stand for 2 hours then cook in spoonfuls in a little fat melted in a frying pan. Turn to cook both sides, and serve hot with castor sugar sprinkled over.

Yorkshire Treacle Tart

rich shortcrust pastry
225g (½ lb) brown
   breadcrumbs
225g (½ lb) mixed dried fruit
1 large cooking apple
1 lemon
2 tablespoons treacle *or* golden
   syrup
a pinch of mixed spice
a pinch of ground ginger

Mix together the spices, mixed dried fruit and breadcrumbs. Squeeze in the juice of the lemon and add the grated rind. Grate the apple, using the peel as well if liked, and add to the mixture. Warm the treacle slightly and pour in, mixing thoroughly.

Line a shallow tin with the pastry, retaining some to lattice the top. Fill with the treacle mixture and cut narrow strips of pastry to arrange over the top in a lattice pattern. Bake in a moderate oven, 180°C (350°F), Gas Mark 4, until the pastry is brown. Serve hot or cold with thick cream.

serves 6.

Ripon Apple Cake

shortcrust pastry
baking apples
sugar *or* golden syrup
grated cheese

This apple cake was customarily served in Ripon during Wilfra Week in August. This week commemorated St Wilfred, the patron saint of the cathedral here. During Wilfra Week the women of the city put an oval dish of jam or lemon cheese tarts just inside their front door for passers-by to enjoy.

Line an ovenproof plate or tin with pastry, retaining enough for a top. Peel and thinly slice the apples and cover the pastry thickly with them. Sweeten to taste with sugar or syrup and sprinkle with grated cheese. Roll out the pastry to make the lid, seal the edges and decorate. Bake in a fairly hot oven, 220°C (425°F), Gas Mark 7, until brown. Sprinkle thickly with castor sugar to serve. Apple pie is traditionally served with cheese in Yorkshire and an old saying is:

> *An apple pie without some cheese*
> *Is like a kiss without a squeeze.*

Rhubarb and Orange Flan

450g (1 lb) forced rhubarb
100g (4 oz) sugar
25g (1 oz) flour
1 beaten egg
grated rind of 1 orange
2 tablespoons orange juice
   made up to 150ml (¼ pint)
   with water
shortcrust pastry

Line a 20-cm (eight-inch) dish or flan ring with slightly sweetened, rich shortcrust pastry. Cut the rhubarb into 2½-cm (1 inch) lengths and place in the dish. Blend sugar, flour, egg and rind. Bring juice to the boil and pour on to the flour mixture, then stir, bring back to the boil (being careful not to let the egg curdle) and strain on to the rhubarb. Decorate with pastry strips. Bake at 220°C (425°F), Gas Mark 7, for 30 minutes.

serves 8

Bilberry Pie

450g (1 lb) bilberries
2 baking apples
shortcrust pastry
75-100 g (3 – 4 oz) castor sugar
2 – 4 tablespoons cold water

Make a cut around the centre of each apple to prevent bursting and put into a dish with a little cold water (not from the 4 tablespoons). Bake at 200°C (400°F), Gas Mark 6, about 40 minutes or until tender. Scrape out the pulp and mix with the bilberries and sugar. Grease a dish and line with pastry, fill with bilberry mixture and sprinkle on the water. Cover with a pastry lid and bake in a hot oven 220°C (425°F), Gas Mark 7 about 20 minutes to cook the pastry, then reduce to 180°C (350°F), Gas Mark 4 until the fruit is tender.

The pastry can be brushed with egg white and sprinkled with castor sugar before cooking if liked and a teaspoonful of cornflour sprinkled over the fruit before the pastry lid is put on will thicken the fruit juice. The apple pulp is not always used but some Yorkshire housewives find that it gives a more moist pie.

serves 6.

North Country Three-Decker Tart

shortcrust pastry
rhubarb, gooseberries, *or* other
    fruit in season
sugar

Line a fireproof dish with pastry and cover with the finely cut fruit. Cover with sugar, then a layer of pastry, next more fruit and sugar and another layer of pastry. Put in one more layer of fruit and sugar, top with pastry and bake in a moderately hot oven, 200°C (400°F), Gas Mark 6, for 45 minutes. Serve with thick cream.

Custard Pie

175g (6 oz) shortcrust pastry
275ml (½ pint) milk
2 eggs
50g (2 oz) sugar
a few drops vanilla essence
grated nutmeg

Custard pie was a traditional dish for Easter Sunday tea in many parts of Yorkshire and especially in the Whitby area, where the name 'custard wind' was given to an easterly wind prevalent there during the Easter period.

Line a greased flan tin or pie dish with pastry. Whisk the eggs and milk well together and stir in the sugar and vanilla essence. Strain into the pastry case and sprinkle on the nutmeg. Bake in a hot oven, 220° – 230°C (425° – 450°F), Gas Mark 7 or 8, for 10 minutes, then turn down to 180°C (350°F), Gas Mark 4, and cook until firm, about 20 minutes.

serves 6.

Butter Curds

575ml (1 pint) new milk
225g (½ lb) butter *or* mar-
    garine
4 eggs
1 teaspoon flour
currants
grated mixed peel
grated nutmeg
a pinch of salt
sugar

This is a Yorkshire recipe of 1873.

'Put the butter and milk into a pan and then heat slowly. Beat the eggs well, add to the milk, and butter when melted. Stir all the time. Mix the flour and salt with a little milk. Stir well until it thickens (not boiling). Then pour into a basin until cold. When cold sweeten to taste with sugar; add a few currants and a little grated nutmeg, also a little grated mixed peal if liked. Line some patty tins with good paste. Add a spoonful of the mixture into each.'

serves 6.

Egg Cheesecakes

4 eggs
175g (6 oz) butter
225g (½ lb) sugar
225g (½ lb) currants
chopped candied peel
rum (optional)
individual pastry cases

This is a Yorkshire recipe from 1873.

'Boil four eggs until hard; shell and place in a basin, and while still warm, add 6 oz good butter, ½lb sugar, ½lb currants, a sprinkling of chopped candied peel, and a flavouring of rum if liked. Chop all together with a knife and fill cases in the usual way.'

makes 36.

Almond Cheesecakes

100g (4 oz) almonds
100g (4 oz) sugar
100g (4 oz) butter
grated rind of 1 lemon
3 eggs
thin puff pastry

'Four ounces of almonds blanched and beaten in a mortar along with four ounces of sugar; add four ounces of butter, the grated rind of a lemon, and three eggs, all beaten well together in a mortar. Put a thin puff paste at the bottom of tins, and insert the mixture.'

This old recipe can be easily adapted by using ground almonds.

Yorkshire Almond Tart

175g (6 oz) pastry
50g (2 oz) sugar
25g (1 oz) butter
2 eggs
25g (1 oz) ground almonds
½ lemon
1 tablespoon castor sugar

This recipe was given to me by a young housewife living in the York area and although this came to her via a relative it is not particularly old.

Beat together the egg yolks, sugar, and the juice and rind of the half lemon. When thick and smooth add the ground almonds and melted butter. Put the bowl over a pan of hot water and stir for ten minutes while the water simmers. By this time the mixture

will be thick. Line a shallow dish or flan tin with the pastry. Pour in the almond mixture and bake at 190°C (375°F), Gas Mark 5, for 30 minutes. Whisk the egg whites until very stiff and dry, spread over the tart and sprinkle the castor sugar over the top. Return to the oven for 8 to 10 minutes, until this meringue has set.

serves 6.

Old-fashioned Syrup Pudding

100g (4 oz) fresh white
   breadcrumbs
75g (3 oz) shredded suet
50g (2 oz) plain flour
1 level teaspoon baking powder
1 lemon
approx. 5 tablespoons cold
   water
100g (4 oz) golden syrup
25g (1 oz) butter

Mix together the suet, baking powder, flour and 75g (3 oz) of the breadcrumbs. Add the grated lemon rind and enough of the water to make a firm suetcrust pastry. Mix the remaining breadcrumbs into the syrup with the lemon juice. Use the butter to grease a basin and fill with alternate layers of pastry and the syrup mixture. Begin with syrup in the bottom of the basin and finish with a pastry topping. Cover securely with either greaseproof paper and a lid, a cloth, or with cooking foil but allow space for expansion. Steam for 3 hours and serve with custard or thick fresh cream.

serves 6.

West Riding Pudding

175g (6 oz) shortcrust pastry
2 tablespoons red jam
100g + 2 dessertspoons (4 oz)
   self-raising flour
100g + 2 dessertspoons (4 oz)
   castor sugar
100g + 1 dessertspoon (4 oz)
   butter
2 eggs
25g (1 oz) ground almonds
grated rind of ½ lemon

Line a shallow dish with the pastry. Decorate the edges and spread the jam on the base. Cream the butter and sugar until light then beat in the eggs gradually. Sift together the dry ingredients and fold these in with further beating. Cover the jam with this mixture and bake in a moderate oven, 180°C (350°F), Gas Mark 4, for 35 to 45 minutes until well risen and firm. Dust with castor sugar.

serves 6.

Harrogate Tart

75g + 1 dessertspoon (3 oz)
   plain flour
50g + ½ dessertspoon (2 oz)
   castor sugar
575ml (1 pint) hot milk
3 egg yolks
1 whole egg
25g (1 oz) butter
75g + 1 dessertspoon (3 oz)
   ground almonds
4 drops almond essence
a little cold milk
a flan case

Mix the flour to a smooth paste with a little cold milk then stir in the yolks, one at a time. Mix in the whole beaten egg and the sugar, stirring very thoroughly. Cut the butter into small pieces and mix into the egg mixture, then add the hot milk. Put the bowl over a pan of hot water, or empty the contents into a double saucepan and cook. Stir constantly, until the mixture is like thick cream. Do not allow it to boil. When thick, remove from the heat and beat in the ground almonds and almond essence. Pour into a baked pastry flan case and serve with fresh cream. The filling can also be used to cover a fruit-filled flan.

serves 6.

Aunty Hannah's Ground Rice Tarts

rich shortcrust pastry:
225g (½ lb) flour
100g + 1 dessertspoon (4 oz) butter
25g (1 oz) sugar
a pinch of salt
cold water

filling:
75g + 1 dessertspoon (3 oz) fine ground rice
40g (1½ oz) ground almonds
75g + ½ dessertspoon (3 oz) sugar
75g + ½ dessertspoon (3 oz) butter
1 large egg
jam

Make shortcrust pastry in the usual way, using the above amounts. Line some small tart tins with the pastry and put half a teaspoon of jam in each. Cream together the butter and sugar. Beat the egg and mix into the ground rice and almonds. Add a little at a time to the creamed mixture. Spread carefully over the jam and bake in a moderate oven 200°C (400°F), Gas Mark 6, until firm, about 20 minutes.

makes 24.

Granny Brown's Currant Pasty

450g (1 lb) flour
200g (7 oz) butter
a pinch of salt
milk
currants
25g (1 oz) fresh mint
1 dessertspoon sugar
granulated sugar

Make pastry using the flour, butter, salt and cold water. Roll into a round and cover one half with currants. Dissolve the sugar in a little boiling water, add the freshly chopped mint and pour evenly over the fruit. Dampen the edges, fold over and seal well. Brush with milk, sprinkle with granulated sugar, prick with a fork and put on a greased oven sheet. Bake in a hot oven until golden brown and crisp.

This can be made in exactly the same way but using finely chopped figs instead of currants. Fig pasties or fig corners as they are sometimes known (depending on the shape) are very popular in Yorkshire.

A rich jam pasty can be made in a similar way but in this case the sugar solution is not used.

makes 12

Paradise Squares

shortcrust pastry
100g + 1 dessertspoon
  (4 oz) castor sugar
100g + 1 dessertspoon
  (4 oz) butter
1 egg
50g + 1 dessertspoon
  (2 oz) ground rice
1 cup sultanas
50g (2 oz) glacé cherries
50g (2 oz) chopped walnuts

Line a shallow 20-cm (eight-inch) square tin with the pastry. Cream the butter and sugar, beat the egg and mix in with the ground rice. Stir in the nuts and fruit and put the mixture into the prepared tin. Smooth the top and bake at 200°C (400°F), Gas Mark 6, until golden brown on top. Remove from the oven and while still warm sprinkle with sugar. Cut into squares when cold.

makes 16.

Mint Pasty

shortcrust pastry
50g (2 oz) sugar
50g (2 oz) butter
75g (3 oz) currants
2 – 3 tablespoons chopped mint

Beat the sugar and butter until creamy then blend in the mint and currants. Roll out the pastry and spread half of it with the mint mixture. Dampen the edges, fold over and seal well. Bake in a hot oven until crisp and brown.

Another method of making this pasty is to use a piece of bread dough, kneading into it half its weight in lard. This is left for 1 hour, then flattened, cut into two, and mint, currants and sugar spread generously upon one portion. Pieces of butter are dotted over the surface which is then covered with the remaining dough and pricked all over before baking in a hot oven.

Cakes, Bread and Biscuits

Cakes, Bread and Biscuits

Home baking is one of the fields in which Yorkshire women seem to excel. The preference for simple, wholesome food in the county combines with inherent thrift to ensure that home-made foods are inevitably more popular than 'shop-bought'.

To see a farmwife's table set for high tea with pies or pasties, home-cured ham, well buttered tea-cakes or oven-bottoms, oatcakes, custard pies, cut-and-come-again cake, parkin and home-made jam and pickles is a perfection in still life.

Dorothy Hartley has stated that Yorkshire tea-cakes, an integral part of a Yorkshire tea, are descended from the manchet bread of medieval times. Now that many women go out to work and rely upon local bakers for bread, cakes and pies, the tradition of home baking is dying out but in Yorkshire most housewives still bake a large proportion of their confectionery. Things like tea-cakes, muffins, crumpets and milk-cakes are, however, now bought in.

In the nineteenth century some women could not bake their own bread although they made it in their homes. Many houses were still without ovens but women did their own cooking and paid a small sum to a local baker to be allowed to use his oven. In 1839 the bellman of Conistone wrote down the message that he was to call out in the village: 'I am to give notige that Jennie Pickersgill yeats yewn to neit, to moarn at mearn, and to moarne at neit, an' nea langer, as lang as storme hods, cos he can git na mare eldin.' Translated from the dialect this reads: 'I am to give notice that Jennie Pickersgill heats oven tonight, tomorrow at morning, and tomorrow at night, and no longer, as long as the storm holds, because she can get no more firewood.'

Records of the last century from Linton and Threshfield show that eight bread bakers and several errand girls lived in the villages, illustrating how, where most of the women worked in local mines and mills, there was a need for bakers and for young girls to run errands.

In medieval days villages often shared communal ovens. One is recorded as having existed at Bainbridge in Wensleydale. Usually, where houses of this period had ovens, they were built into the thickness of the walls or sometimes extended outside the house. Some of these early ovens survive and are known as beehive ovens because of their interior shape.

Where a home had an open fire but no oven a kail pot hung above the fire for boiling the family's basic pottage but this could also be used for baking certain foods. Then it would be stood upon the hearth and hot peat piled around and upon it, the heat baking the rough bread inside. By the eighteenth century many homes had some kind of hob grate for burning coals which still had a black pot hanging above it with, in Yorkshire, a portable bakestone standing close by for the cooking of oatcakes. Three types of bakestone were quarried to be sold and hawked around Yorkshire to be placed over the fire for oatcake-baking

In the mid-nineteenth century a writer described the improvements which had gradually been introduced into baking: 'Among these is the use of an oven heated by a furnace exterior to it, instead of by fuel introduced into the oven itself.' This was regarded as a great innovation for the oven had previously to be heated by the burning wood, sticks and twigs with which it was filled, the door being closed and the oven left until the wood had burned away. The ash was quickly swept out and bread thrust into the hot oven. Sometimes the loaves were put on racks which had been made by the local blacksmith so that two or more layers of bread could be baked. The small round cakes of dough which sat on the floor of the oven were known as oven-bottoms and are still sold by Yorkshire bakers.

In Anglo-Saxon times barley, rye or oatbread were the only types eaten in Yorkshire. Harrison wrote in Tudor times: 'The bread throughout the land is made of such graine as the soil yieldeth; neverthelesse the gentilitie commonlie provide themselves with rie and barlie; yea, and in time of dearth, maine with bread made either of bran, peasen, or otes, or of altogether.'

The household book of the Duke of Northumberland listed in 1512 the amounts and prices of food consumed at his two Yorkshire homes. At breakfast one day, 'For my Lord and my Lady. A loaf of bread in trenchers, 2 manchettes, 1 quart of beer, a quart of wine, half a chine of mutton, or elles a chine of beef boil'd.'

Sir Edmund Coke's household book of 1596 listed 'otmell to make the poore folkes porage—riemell to make breads for the poore.'

Oatmeal has always been well liked in Yorkshire since early times when oatbread was the only kind available to the poor. Oats were not only used to make 'six several kinds of good and wholesome bread' as according to Markham in 1615, but were used in meat pottage, milk pottage and gruel, as well as to make the oatcakes now regarded as traditional in Yorkshire. Markham described oats as the 'very crown of the housewife's garland' and probably it is this long-standing tradition which has given Yorkshirewomen their understanding of the qualities of oats, leading them to create such favourites as parkin and moggy as well as a variety of oaten biscuits and cakes.

Two sorts of oatcake were made, the first from a dough which was rolled out and cooked on a bakestone and was known as haverbread or havercake, or sometimes as clapbread from the old way of clapping the dough on to the hollowed board by hand during the preparation. Oatcake or riddlebread was made from a yeast batter and poured or tossed on to a bakestone. (See page 123 for a traditional recipe.) By 1883 A. Easther was to write in *A Glossary of the Dialect of Almondbury and Huddersfield* that 'Oatcake is seldom made by any but public bakers.' This was probably true but in some country districts oatcakes are still made by elderly people in the traditional way. Commercial oatcake bakers had opened shops in most towns by the end of last century, having huge cast-iron bakestones installed. One of these can be seen in Keighley at the Cliffe Castle Museum. And it is still possible to find bakers using the old way of oatcake making. Here also is an old waffle-making iron. Waffles were made in the early nineteenth century in the north of England and Scotland; a waffle iron of this period was found in Bradford some years ago.

Commercial bakers sold the crumpets, muffins and milk cakes loved by all Yorkshire people. It is rare to find a village without a shop where one can buy these and most markets have a stall where they are sold. Those markets always seem most popular where 'home-made' foodstuffs can be bought and Yorkshire is very well endowed with talented housewives who share their baking with others from stalls set up weekly in country markets.

Gingerbread was originally nothing more than a ginger-flavoured slab of honey and breadcrumbs, frequently made as a gift in early medieval days. It was sometimes gilded with gold leaf and decorated with cloves. Both gingerbread and parkin have been made in Yorkshire for centuries, with many variations, and moggy is one of these variants. Sometimes described as a 'flour parkin', moggy became traditional harvest-time fare; the name is thought to derive from the Old Norse 'mugi', a heap of corn. For a selection of recipes see pages 112 and 113.

Many traditional cakes and biscuits were associated with religious festivals or seasons of the year. Local specialities were sold as fairings, such as the brandy snaps sold at Hull Fair, first held in 1279. For a brandy snap recipe see page 124.

Pepper Cake, known in some parts of the country as Spice Bread or Cake, was a Christmas speciality and would always be offered to carol singers or any callers during the Christmas period. You will find a recipe on page 114. It is still customary to offer cheese with the Christmas Cake or Yule Cake in Yorkshire.

Custard pies were traditionally served on Easter Sunday, especially in the Whitby area, but they were also Whitsuntide fare in other parts of the county. One very popular cake once traditional to Whitsun is the Yorkshire

Curd Tart or Cheesecake. The earliest type of curd tart was probably Beestings Tart, made from milk taken from a newly calved cow. This continues to be made and is incredibly rich. Andrew Boorde wrote in the sixteenth century: 'Take new cheese, and grynde hit fayne, in mortar with eggs—Put powder thereto of sugar coloure hit with Safrone. Put hit in cofyns that be fayre, and bake it forthe.' New cheese was an ancient Yorkshire delicacy made from beestings, diluted with milk and sweetened with honey. Still made, but usually now sweetened with syrup.

Farmwives also use beestings thinned with an equal amount of water and with milk added, the whole is heated to make curds for using in curd tarts, great tea-time favourites. (See page 118 for a recipe).

Fruit cake or cut-and-come-again cake has always been well regarded and is one of the essential ingredients of a typical high tea. Some delicious recipes are to be found on pages 117-188. I like to think that this fondness evolved from the canniness or carefulness attributed to Yorkshire people. When ovens were heated interiorly, bread would be the first item baked, pies next and as the oven cooled, small buns or sponge cakes might be baked. Perhaps a corner was always found for a cut-and-come-again cake when the first pie was cooked, the cake remaining in the oven throughout the rest of the baking period. So a cake that would last all week could be made by using the nature of a cooling oven to the greatest advantage.

Afternoon tea became fashionable during the 1850s with the combined influences of the discovery of Indian tea in Assam in 1823 and the invention of a successful baking powder in America in the late 1840s. Middle-class hostesses vied with each other in producing the most delicate biscuits and teas. Among the artisans and farm labourers, high tea became a popular full meal to be eaten after work. In Yorkshire this innovation of the late nineteenth century coincided with the temperance movement and the meal became a valued type of church gathering. Biscuits, originally a form of bread rusk split and rebaked until crisp, were usually either oat or ginger as north country people have always been most partial to these; and sad cakes, those currant and pastry slices still widespread in the north under a variety of names, were often featured. They evolved in the days when fruit was difficult to cultivate and dried fruit became the most common sweet filling for pastry cases. (See pages 117 and 124 for recipes.)

With the usual selection of pies and pickles, generously buttered plain and currant tea-cakes, malt bread, curd tarts and cups of tea, the high tea table is ready.

CAKES

Aunty Belle's Parkin

150g + 1½ dessertspoons (6 oz)
  self-raising flour
150g + 3 dessertspoons (6 oz)
  oatmeal *or* oats
100g + 1 dessertspoon
  (4 oz) soft brown sugar
75g + ½ dessertspoon (3 oz)
  golden syrup
25g (1 oz) black treacle
100g + 1 dessertspoon (4 oz)
  butter
1 egg
½ cup milk
½ teaspoon bicarbonate of
  soda
2 teaspoons ground ginger
a pinch of salt

Put the flour, ginger, oatmeal and salt into a bowl. Gently melt together the sugar, syrup, treacle and butter and pour over the flour mixture. Beat the egg and stir into the milk. Add the bicarbonate of soda and beat lightly, then pour into the bowl with the other ingredients. Mix thoroughly and pour into a prepared shallow tin. If liked a little of the beaten egg can be kept to brush over the parkin before baking to give a glaze.

Bake in a moderate oven, 180°C (350°F), Gas Mark 4, for 1 hour or until firm. Keep wrapped for a few days before using.

Treacle Parkin

1.4kg (3 lb) oatmeal
325g + 2 dessertspoons
  (¾ lb) sugar
225g (½ lb) butter
100g + 1 dessertspoon (¼ lb)
  lard
900g (2 lb) treacle
50g + 1 dessertspoon (2 oz)
  ginger
lemon
powdered cinnamon
3 tablespoons ale *or* brandy

This 1804 recipe of Elizabeth Shillito is taken from Margaret Walker's *Cookery and Commonplace Book,* 1778-1846, in the University of Leeds library, Blanche Leigh Collection.

'3 lbs Oatmeal; ¾ lb sugar; ½ lb Butter; ¼ lb lard; 2 lb Treacle; 2 oz ginger; Lemon, Powdered cinnamon to your taste. 3 Tablespoons of Ale or Brandy. Bake it in loaves.'

This recipe gives a more closely textured parkin than is favoured today when a mixture of oatmeal and flour is used. A blend of treacle and syrup is also used in parkin-making now but in earlier times both gingerbread and parkin were made entirely with treacle.

Moggy

675g + 1 dessertspoon
 (1½ lbs) plain flour
225g (½ lb) sugar
225g (½ lb) golden syrup
150g + 1½ dessertspoons
 (6 oz) butter
150g + 1½ dessertspoons
 (6 oz) lard
3 teaspoons baking powder
a pinch of salt
milk to mix *or* egg and milk

Moggy Parkin is simply referred to as Moggy in some districts, the word Moggy being traced back through Early English where corn was known as 'muge', later 'muga'. In Old Norse a heap of corn was 'mugi'.

Sieve together the flour, baking powder and salt. Rub in the fats. Add the sugar and syrup, then mix to a stiff dough with the milk, or a beaten egg and a little milk, for added richness. Cut into two pieces and roll each one to a 1¼ cm (a half-inch) thickness. Place on a greased baking tray and bake in a moderate oven until firm, about 25 minutes. Cut into squares when cold.

Granny's Moggy Parkin

675g + 1 dessertspoon
 (1½ lbs) flour
450g (1 lb) treacle
50g + ½ dessertspoon (2 oz)
 sugar
50g + ½ dessertspoon
 (2 oz) butter
50g + ½ dessertspoon (2 oz)
 lard
1 egg
½ cup milk
1 teaspoon bicarbonate of soda
1 teaspoon cream of tartar
1 teaspoon ground ginger
½ – 1 teaspoon salt

Mix as for the parkin recipe above but bake in a deep tin for about 1½ hours or until firm to the touch, at 160°C (325°F), Gas Mark 3.

Parkin has been a traditional feature of Plot Night (5 November) Yorkshire for many years and particularly in the West Riding. It has a certain similarity with a Lancashire speciality called Harcake, said to have originated in pagan times.

Gingerbread

800g (1 lb 12 oz) flour
350g (12 oz) honey
100g (4 oz) butter
½ teaspoon baking powder
15g (½ oz) ground ginger
½ level teaspoon ground
 nutmeg

This recipe has been modernized to some extent but is probably very similar in texture and flavour to the earliest types of gingerbread.

Melt the honey gently with two tablespoons of water. Cut the butter into small pieces and add to the honey. When the butter has melted, blend together all the ingredients very thoroughly. Press into buttered moulds or tins to a depth of 2½ cm (one inch). Bake for 20 minutes at 150°C (300°F), Gas Mark 2.

York Gingerbread

1.1kg (2½ lb) stale bread
900g (2lb) fine powder (castor)
    sugar
25g (1 oz) cinnamon
2 tablespoons mace
2 tablespoons ginger
1 tablespoon sanders
100g + 2 dessertspoons (4 oz)
    almonds
275ml (½ pint) red wine
3 spoonfuls brandy
cinnamon
1 tablespoon ground cloves

This recipe comes from Sarah Martin's book *The New Experienced English Housekeeper* (1800). Sanders, the red colouring matter from sandalwood, is no longer available and is only included for historical interest.

'Take two pounds and a half of stale bread grated fine but not dried, two pounds of fine powder sugar, an ounce of cinnamon, half an ounce of mace, half an ounce of ginger, a quarter of an ounce of sanders, and a quarter of a pound of almonds, boil the sugar, sanders, ginger and mace in half a pint of red wine, then put in three spoonsful of brandy, a little cinnamon and a quarter of an ounce of cloves. Stir in half the bread, on the fire, but do not let it boil, pour it out and work in the rest of the bread with the almonds then smother it close half an hour, make it into cakes about an inch thick, and bake them quarter of an hour, keep dry.'

Mrs Gott's Seed Cake

225g (½ lb) self-rasing
    flour
100g + 1 dessertspoon (4 oz)
    sugar
100g + 1 dessertspoon
    (4 oz) butter
3 eggs
2 tablespoons milk
1 dessertspoon caraway seeds

Beat the sugar and butter together until light and creamy. Whisk the eggs and milk together. Stir the seeds into the flour and alternately add to the creamed mixture with the liquid, a little at a time. Blend well then put into a 20-cm (8-inch) prepared tin and bake in a moderate oven for 45 minutes or until firm and golden brown.

Pepper Cake

325g + 2 dessertspoons (¾ lb)
    plain flour
325g + 1 dessertspoon
    (¾ lb) black treacle
100g + 1 dessertspoon (4 oz)
    soft brown sugar
100g + 1 dessertspoon (4 oz)
    butter *or* margarine
2 beaten eggs
¾ teaspoon bicarbon-
    ate of soda
2 tablespoons ground cloves
8 tablespoons milk

This was a Christmas speciality, given to carol-singers and any visitor. The spice gave it its peppery taste. The Christmas Waits often ended their singing with the verse:

> *A little bit of pepper cake,*
> *A little bit of cheeese.*
> *A little drink of water*
> *And a penny, if you please!*

Rub the fat into the flour; add the sugar and spice. Mix the bicarbonate of soda with the milk and add to the flour with the treacle and eggs. Mix all together thoroughly and put into a 25-cm (10-in), well-greased and lined tin. Bake until firm in a moderate oven for between 50 and 60 minutes.

Redcar Cake

325g + 2 dessertspoons
    (¾ lb) flour
225g (½ lb) castor sugar
225g (½ lb) butter
3 eggs
50g + 1 dessertspoon (2 oz)
    ground almonds
1 teaspoon baking powder
milk
chopped almonds

Cream together the butter and sugar. Beat in the eggs one at a time. Sieve together the flour, ground almonds and baking powder and blend thoroughly into the butter mixture. Add a little milk if needed to give a firm dropping consistency. Place in a greased tin, 30cm x 20cm (12in x 8in), then sprinkle with chopped nuts and bake at 190°C (375°F), Gas Mark 5, until firm.

Hessle Spice

550g + 2 dessertspoons
    (1¼ lb) flour
325g + 1 dessertspoon (¾ lb)
    sugar
2 scant tablespoons treacle
150g + 1 dessertspoon
    (6 oz) margarine
50g + ½ dessertspoon
    (2 oz) lard
100g (4 oz) raisins
2 eggs
225g (½ lb) currants
50g (2 oz) blanched almonds
1 rounded teaspoon baking
    powder
1 scant teaspoon bicarbonate of
    soda
milk
50g (2 oz) mixed candied peel

Sieve together the flour and baking powder; rub in the fats. Chop the nuts and peel, then add them to the flour mixture with the sugar. Warm a little milk and in it dissolve the bicarbonate of soda. Beat the eggs and blend in the treacle. Combine the milk and eggs with the flour, fruit, etc. Blend well and add more milk if necessary to give a firm dropping consistency. Bake in a slow oven, 160°C (325°F), Gas Mark 3, until brown and set. This might take 2½ to 3 hours.

Love Feast Cake

450g (1 lb) flour
225g (½ lb) sugar
125g + 1 dessertspoon (5 oz)
    half butter and half lard
2 small eggs
225g (½ lb) currants
25g (1 oz) candied peel
25g (1 oz) baking powder
1 – 2 teaspoons mixed spice

During the eighteenth century, Love Feasts became popular in districts converted to Methodism, where they were held four times a year. A two-handled cup was passed around for all to share, together with slices of Love Feast Cake which derived its name from this gathering in love and fellowship.

Mix together the flour, baking powder and mixed spice. Rub in the fats. Beat the eggs and chop the candied peel finely. Add the fruit, peel and sugar to the rubbed-in mixture and mix in the eggs. Put into the prepared tin and bake in a moderate oven until firm to the touch.

Bedale Plum Cake

125g + 2 dessertspoons
  (5 oz) flour
100g + 1 dessertspoon (4 oz)
  Demerara sugar
100g + 1 dessertspoon
  (4 oz) butter
2 eggs
50g (2 oz) currants
50g (2 oz) raisins
25g (1 oz) candied peel
½ lemon
1 teaspoon baking powder
½ teaspoon mixed spice

Sieve together the flour, baking powder and spice. Chop the candied peel and beat the eggs. Grate the lemon rind and squeeze out the juice. Cream together the butter and sugar. Mix together dried fruits, lemon rind and dry ingredients. Pour the lemon juice into the eggs. Add the egg mixture to the creamed butter and sugar, alternately with the fruit and flour. Beat together very thoroughly then put into the prepared tin. Bake in a moderate oven, 180°C (350°F), Gas Mark 4, for 1 hour or until firm.

Mell Cake or Pig-Killing Cake

225g (½ lb) flour
25g (1 oz) Demerara sugar
50g + 1 dessertspoon (2 oz)
  butter
50g + ½ dessertspoon (2 oz)
  lard
50 – 75g (2 – 3 oz) currants
ground nutmeg
butter
soft brown sugar

Mell Cake was traditionally made to serve at the celebratory supper held on the evening of pig-killing day. The word Mell is derived from the Danish word for a meal.

Rub the fats into the flour until the mixture has a breadcrumb-like consistency. Add the currants and Demerara sugar, then mix to a firm dough with a little water. Roll out to 2 cm (three-quarter-inch) thickness and place on a greased oven sheet. Bake in a fairly hot oven until golden brown and split open while hot. Spread with butter, sprinkle with soft brown sugar and add a pinch of nutmeg. Sandwich together again and spread the top with butter, sugar and nutmeg. Serve immediately.

Old Wife's Cake

450g (1lb) flour
225g (½ lb) sugar
225g (½ lb) butter
225g (½ lb) currants
1 tablespoon milk
1 teaspoon bicarbonate soda
½ grated nutmeg
a little lemon juice (optional)

Old Wife's Cake was traditionally eaten during the Christmas period.

Cream the butter and sugar, then add the currants, flour and bicarbonate of soda. Mix in the grated nutmeg and the lemon juice. Stir in the milk and mix well. Pat lightly into well-buttered tins and bake until lightly browned in a moderate oven. This amount will fill three small 15-cm (6-inch) tins.

Mrs Gott's Fruit Cake

225g (½ lb) plain flour
100g + 1 dessertspoon (4 oz)
    soft brown sugar
1 tablespoon of honey
1 teaspoon treacle
150g + 1½ dessertspoons
    (6 oz) butter
5 eggs
350g (¾ lb) currants
100g (4 oz) cherries (glacé)
50g + 1 dessertspoon (2 oz)
    ground almonds
the grated rind from 2 oranges
the grated rind from 1 lemon
1 dessertspoon ground
    cinnamon
½ teaspoon ground ginger
a few drops of almond essence
wineglass of sherry

This cake is suitable for weddings and other festive family occasions.

Cream the butter and sugar, then add the honey and treacle. Sift together plain flour, ground ginger, ground almond and cinnamon and add alternately with the beaten eggs to the sugar and butter mixture. Stir in the prepared fruit, rinds, chopped cherries and essence. Mix thoroughly and put into a well-lined 18-cm (7-inch) tin. Bake in a moderate oven for 1½ hours, until firm.

Store in an airtight tin after pouring a wineglassful of sherry over the top. If the cake is to be kept for some time turn the cake over and make a series of holes with a skewer and pour a little sherry over the bottom each week.

Yorkshire Curd Tarts

225g (8 oz) curds
2 eggs
75g (3 oz) sugar
50g (2 oz) currants
25g (1 oz) butter
the grated rind of ½ lemon
a pinch of nutmeg
150g (6 oz) shortcrust
    pastry

Mix the curds, currants, lemon rind and nutmeg thoroughly together. Beat the eggs and add. Melt the butter and add with the sugar. Line a dish or plate with the pastry and put in the curd mixture. Bake in a moderate oven, 180°C (350°F), Gas Mark 4, for twenty minutes or until set.

Yule Cake

657g + 1 dessertspoon
    (1½ lbs) self-rasing
    flour
225g (½ lb) soft brown sugar
325g + 1 dessertspoon (¾ lb)
    butter
3 eggs
225g (½ lb) currants
225g (½ lb) raisins

Fruit cakes played an essential part in the Christmas festivities and recipes still abound for Yule Cakes in many parts of the north of England. This cake was traditionally served during the Christmas period in the Whitby area, often accompanied by a glass of cherry brandy.

Mix together the flour, brown sugar, nutmeg and cinnamon. Add the nuts, fruit and chopped candied peel. Rub the butter into the flour. Beat the eggs and add the brandy. Add the dry

100g (4 oz) candied peel
50g (2 oz) chopped almonds
1 teaspoon each of ground
    nutmeg and cinnamon
1 glass brandy
cream

ingredients to the creamed mixture alternately with the eggs. Work into a dough with a little cream and press into a large, shallow tin. Mark off into small squares, cutting only halfway down.

Bake at 160°C (325°F), Gas Mark 3, until firm. This will take about 2½ hours. Remove from the tin when cooked and when the cake is cold break it into rough squares.

BREAD

Ripon Spice Bread

450g (1 lb) plain flour
125g + 1 dessertspoon
    (5 oz) sugar
100g + 1 dessertspoon (4 oz)
    butter
100g + 1 dessertspoon
    (4 oz) lard
1 egg
425ml (¾ pint) milk
225g (½ lb) mixed dried fruit
25g (1 oz) candied peel
1 level dessertspoon (½ oz)
    fresh yeast
1 level teaspoon sugar
2 level teaspoons mixed spice
a good pinch of salt

Put the flour and salt in a large bowl in a warm place. Rub in the fats. Cream the yeast with the teaspoonful of sugar, beat the egg and mix these together. Warm the milk to blood heat and stir into the flour with the yeast mixture. Mix well, cover with a slightly dampened cloth and leave in a warm place for an hour. Turn out and knead thoroughly, working in the fruit, peel, sugar and spices. Put into two buttered and floured 450g (1 lb) tins. Leave to prove in a warm place for 25 minutes covered with a clean cloth. Bake in a hot oven 230°C (450°F), Gas Mark 4, for approximately 50 minutes

Buttermilk Bread

1½kg (3½ lb) flour
675g + 1 dessertspoon
    (1½ lbs) moist brown sugar
325g + 1 dessertspoon (12 oz)
    lard
buttermilk
450g (1 lb) raisins
450g (1 lb) currants
100g (4 oz) chopped mixed
    peel
1 tablespoon bicarbonate of
    soda
1 teaspoon salt

This old recipe gives large quantities and perhaps half these amounts will be enough.

Sieve the flour and salt, rub in the lard. Add the sugar, raisins, currants and peel. Dissolve the bicarbonate of soda in a little buttermilk and add to the mixture with enough extra buttermilk to make a slack dough. Knead lightly and put into the prepared bread tins. Bake in a moderately hot oven for 2½ to 3 hours, until the loaves are firm and the bottoms sound hollow when tapped.

makes 4 loaves.

York Mayne Bread

325g + 2 dessertspoons
    (¾ lb) flour
225g (½ lb) sugar
3 egg yolks
2 egg whites
a third of a cup of milk and
    water mixed
1 level dessertspoon (½ oz)
    yeast
1 teaspoon coriander seed
1 teaspoon caraway seeds
2 teaspoons rose water

Mayne bread was made in York for distinguished visitors to the city during the period 1445 to 1662, but the recipe has not been preserved. In 1950 the following recipe was discovered in an old manuscript and used to make Mayne Bread during the 1951 York Festival.

Heat the milk and water mixture until tepid and stir in the yeast. Mix the egg yolks into the rosewater. Blend the flour, sugar and seeds. Combine the yeast and rosewater mixtures with the flour. Beat the whites until stiff and stir in. Mix well, then put to prove in a warm place for 20 to 25 minutes. Knead lightly and shape. Prove for a further 10 minutes. Bake in a moderate oven until golden brown. This will only take between 10 and 15 minutes if the bread is shaped into small rolls.

White Bread

1kg 350gm (3 lb) strong flour
1 litre (1¾ pints) milk and
    water mixed
25g (1 oz) yeast
25g (1 oz) salt
25g (1 oz) soft brown sugar

Mix the yeast and sugar together and leave in a warm place until creamy. Put the salt with half the flour into a warm bowl and add the creamed yeast mixture. Heat the milk and water until blood heat or tepid, then pour into the bowl and mix until as smooth as possible. Cover and leave in a warm place to prove for 15 minutes. Stir in the remaining flour which should have been kept warm and work until smooth. Knead this dough for 10 to 15 minutes then place into warm, greased 450g (1 lb) loaf tins. Cover with a slightly dampened cloth and leave to prove for 45 minutes. Bake in a hot oven until cooked and the bottom of each loaf sounds hollow when tapped. This will take approximately 45 minutes at 200°C (450°F), Gas Mark 7 or 8. This amount will make four loaves.

Quick Wholewheat Bread

450g (1 lb) wholewheat flour
275ml (½ pint) warm water
15g (½ oz) fresh yeast or
    1 tablespoon dried
1 teaspoon sugar
1 dessertspoon oil
1 teaspoon salt

Mix together the yeast, sugar and a little of the tepid water and leave in a warm place until creamy. Mix the dry ingredients in a warm bowl, then add the liquid, yeast and oil. Mix thoroughly until a smooth firm dough is obtained, adding more water if necessary. Put into a warmed and greased 900g (2 lb) loaf tin and cover with a slightly dampened cloth. Leave in a warm place to prove for 30 minutes. Bake in a hot oven until cooked and firm (test as for white bread), about 30 minutes at 200°C (400°F), Gas Mark 6.

Little Cakes and Biscuits

Scarborough Muffins

775g + 3 dessertspoons
  (1¾ lbs) flour
575ml (1 pint) milk
2 eggs
50 g (2 oz) fresh yeast
1 teaspoon sugar
a good pinch of salt

Muffins, called in some districts oven-bottom cakes, share popularity with milk cakes and crumpets in most small confectioners' shops. Muffins were made by most housewives until this century, usually on bread-baking day, as the muffins consisted simply of pieces of bread dough which were flattened and baked on the floor of the oven or in special round moulds placed on a bakestone or on the oven floor. A hole was traditionally made in the centre of each muffin before baking, and the cakes are never cut but pulled apart to be spread with butter. Scarborough muffins are a richer version of the traditional type.

Blend the yeast and sugar. Leave in a warm place until creamy. Warm the milk to blood heat and pour in the beaten eggs. Mix together the flour and salt then pour in the milk and the yeast mixture to make a firm dough. Knead lightly then pat out and cut into rounds. Put on an oven tray and leave to prove for 30 minutes. Bake until firm, about 20 to 30 minutes at 220°C (425°F), Gas Mark 7.

makes 12

Cheese Muffins

1½ cups flour
½ cup grated cheese
1 egg
¾ cup milk
2 teaspoons baking powder
a good pinch of salt

Beat together the eggs and milk. Sieve the dry ingredients into a bowl. Stir in the cheese and pour in the liquid, and beat well to make a workable dough. Roll out to 2½ cm (1 inch) thickness and cut into rounds. Put on a greased baking sheet and bake in a hot oven for 10 minutes or until well risen and browned. Cut into halves, butter thickly and serve hot.

Yorkshire Teacakes

450g (1 lb) flour
25g (1 oz) sugar
25g (1 oz) lard
275 – 425ml (½ – ¾ pint)
  warm milk

Sieve the flour and salt, rub in the lard and leave in a warm place. Put the yeast and one teaspoonful of sugar into a dish to cream. Add the fruit and sugar to the warmed flour, then make a well in the centre and pour in the yeast mixture with some of the milk warmed to blood heat. Mix lightly, and gradually add more milk

50g (2 oz) currants or mixed
    currants and sultanas
25g (1 oz) yeast
1 teaspoon sugar
1 teaspoon salt

to make a soft dough. Beat well until smooth. Cover the basin with a clean cloth and leave in a warm place to rise for about 1 hour. Turn out on to a floured board and knead well. Divide into six portions, kneading each one and rolling it out flat. Place on a greased baking sheet. Leave to rise until doubled in bulk and spongy. Bake until golden brown in a fairly hot oven 220°C (425°F), Gas Mark 7, for 10 to 15 minutes.

makes 6.

Plain Yorkshire Teacakes

675g (1½ lb) flour
425ml (¾ pint) milk and water
    mixed
50g (2 oz) lard
25g (1 oz) sugar
25g (1 oz) yeast
½ teaspoon salt

Mix the flour and salt in a warm bowl and rub in the lard. Cream the yeast and sugar and warm the liquid (milk and water) to blood heat. Mix together the yeast and liquid, pour into the bowl and mix well with the flour, etc. Knead lightly in the bowl for 7 to 10 minutes, then cover and leave in a warm place to prove for 30 minutes. Divide into 12 pieces and knead each one lightly so it is formed into a neat cake. Put on to warm greased baking trays and cover with a light cloth. Leave to prove a further 30 minutes, then bake in a hot oven for 7 to 10 minutes.

makes 12.

Grandma Clarke's Scones

450g (1 lb) self-rasing
    flour
150g + 1½ dessertspoons
    (6 oz) castor sugar
125g + 1 dessertspoon (5 oz)
    butter
2 small eggs
2 tablespoons milk
50g (2 oz) currants
½ teaspoon baking powder
a pinch of salt

Mix together all the dry ingredients and rub in the butter. Add the currants and sugar. Beat the eggs and add with just enough of the milk to make a stiff dough. Roll out to 2½ cm (an inch) thickness, cut into small rounds and put on to a greased oven sheet. Bake in a hot oven, 230°C (450°F), Gas Mark 8, until well risen and brown. This will take about 15 minutes. Serve cut open and well buttered but for a special occasion they are recommended also with jam and whipped cream.

makes 18

Funeral Biscuits

5½kg (12 lbs) flour
4kg (9 lbs) sifted sugar
4½kg (10 lbs) butter
3 teaspoons baking powder
1 small teaspoon bicarbonate of
    soda
caraway seeds

Known also as funeral biskeys, tuppenny cakes or funeral bread, depending upon the type made in the area, these were customarily given to mourners after a funeral. Sometimes like a tea-cake, frequently made with caraway seeds, funeral biscuits were usually impressed with a pattern if made at home. When bought from a shop advertising 'Funeral biscuits a speciality' they were usually spongy in texture rather than like shortbread, as the home-made ones tended to be.

The following recipe is a traditional one and gives enormous quantities. You will probably have to omit the stamp.

Rub the butter into the sieved and combined dry ingredients. Add the caraway seeds. Knead lightly and weight out 125g (five ounces) of dough for each cake. Shape each cake into a round and press with the patterned stamp.

makes 100.

Traditional Oatcake

675g (1½ lbs) fine oatmeal
15g (½ oz) fresh yeast
575ml (1 pint) warm water
½ – 1 teaspoon salt

'Combine all the ingredients gently, mixing with the hands to make a smooth batter. Cover and leave in a warm place for 30 minutes to prove. Shake coarse oatmeal over a board and pour on enough batter to cover, shake the board gently to shape the oatcake, then, with a flick of the wrist, throw the oatcake into a long oval on the heated backstone (or griddle).'

Oatcakes

225g (½ lb) medium oatmeal
225g (½ lb) flour
100g + 1 dessertspoon (4 oz) lard
1 teaspoon salt
cold water

Oatmeal is still very popular in Yorkshire, the plentiful piles of oatcakes on stalls in almost every market bearing witness to this fact. Few women make the traditional type of oatcake at home but there are adaptations which are widely used. This recipe is one of these.

Combine the flour, oatmeal and salt. Rub in the lard and mix to a firm paste with cold water. Roll out on a board sprinkled with oatmeal until very thin, then cut into shapes. Alternatively, the dough can be divided into small balls before rolling, each will then make one oatcake.

Bake on an ungreased griddle until firm; only one side is cooked.

makes 36

Oaty Biscuits

25g (9 oz) bread dough
100g (4 oz) lard
225g (8 oz) porridge oats
100g (4 oz) sugar
1 teaspoon baking powder

An unusual kind of biscuit that is still greatly liked in Yorkshire and can be made from a piece of bread dough

Keep back a piece of bread dough, weighing about 250 g (9 oz) after bread baking. Rub the lard into the porage oats and stir in the sugar and baking powder. Knead this mixture thoroughly into the dough. Roll out to about ½ cm (¼ inch) thick and cut into squares. Bake at 160 – 180°C (325 – 350°F), Gas Mark 3 – 4, until just firm but not too crisp.

makes 36

Oatmeal Biscuits

100g + 2 dessertspoons (4 oz)
  flour
75g + ½ dessertspoon (3 oz)
  butter
1 egg
25g (1 oz) castor sugar
  (optional)
a pinch of salt and baking
  powder
150g + 3 dessertspoons
  (6 oz) medium or fine
  oatmeal

Mix together the flour, salt and baking powder. Rub in the butter and add the oatmeal and sugar, if used. Beat the egg and add to make a firm dough, using a little water if necessary. Roll out thinly and cut into rounds. Put onto a greased oven sheet and bake very slowly until lightly brown. This will take 25 minutes at 140°C (275°F), Gas Mark 1.

makes 24.

Brandy Snaps

50g + 1 dessertspoon (2 oz)
  flour
50g + ½ dessertspoon
  (2 oz) castor sugar
50g + ½ dessertspoon (2 oz)
  golden syrup
50g + ½ dessertspoon (2 oz)
  butter
½ – 1 teaspoon ground ginger
1 teaspoon brandy (optional)

Brandy snaps have been a traditional fairing at Hull Fair for many centuries. This Fair dates back to 1279 when the town was called Wyke. The name was changed to Kingston-upon-Hull in 1293.

Melt the butter and stir in the syrup and sugar. Remove from the heat and add the remaining ingredients gradually. Mix well. Drop small spoonfuls of the mixture on to a buttered baking sheet. Space at least 7½cm (3 inches) apart to allow for spreading.

Bake at 200°C (400°F), Gas Mark 6, for 10 minutes until set. Allow to cool on the sheet for a minute or two until the Brandy Snaps can be lifted off easily with a palette knife. Curl around the greased handle of a wooden spoon to shape before they cool.

makes 18

Yorkshire Fat Rascals

450g (1 lb) plain flour
225g (½ lb) butter
50g + ½ dessertspoon (2 oz)
  brown sugar
100g (4 oz) currants
salt
castor sugar
milk and water

Fat Rascals were known as Turf Cakes on the moorland areas near Whitby where they were cooked on a griddle over an open turf or peat fire.

Rub the butter into the flour, then add the currants, brown sugar and salt. Mix in enough milk and water to make a slack dough. Roll out to 1cm (half-inch) thickness, cut into rounds and dust with castor sugar. Put on to a greased baking tin and bake in a fairly hot oven until golden brown.

Melting Moments

275g + 1 dessertspoon
(10 oz) flour
225g (½ lb) sugar
225g (½ lb) margarine
1 teaspoon baking powder
crushed cornflakes
a few glacé cherries

These biscuits are made by Mrs Greenwood and sold from her stall in Ripon market.

Beat the sugar and margarine together until very light and creamy. Mix the flour and baking powder and work in to margarine mixture to give a shortbread-type mixture. Roll into small balls and dip into the cornflakes. Flatten slightly and press a small piece of cherry on each biscuit. Bake at 180°C (350°F), Gas Mark 4, until golden brown, then leave to cool on the tin. Space out before cooking as the biscuits tend to spread.

makes 48.

Tom Trot

225g (½ lb) Demerara sugar
225g (½ lb) black treacle
100g (4 oz) butter

This dark toffee is called Plot Toffee in some parts of Yorkshire where it is traditionally served on Bonfire Plot Night, 5th November.

Melt the butter and add the treacle and sugar. Simmer gently for 30 minutes then test for setting in cold water. When a hard set is reached, (that is, when a small quantity put into a saucer of cold water forms a thin brittle film and cracks easily), pour into a well-buttered tin and leave to cool.

In Bottle
and Jar

In Bottle and Jar

Blackcurrant Tea

1 tablespoon blackcurrant jam
1 slice lemon
275ml (½ pint) boiling water

This typical North Country remedy for colds was taken from a book belonging to the Shipley family, dated 1884.

'Put a tablespoonof blackcurrant jam in a jug with a slice of lemon and half a pint of boiling water. Stir well and stand until cold. Strain and use as a drink for colds.'

Gale Beer

4½ litres (1 gallon) water
1kg (2 lbs) sugar
1 large bunch gale (bog myrtle)
½ lemon
1 teaspoon cream of tartar
1 slice toast
25g (1 oz) fresh yeast

Gale beer has been a traditional Yorkshire brew for centuries, the suggestion having been put forward that it was made in the monastery of Whitby. In more recent times it was made on farms to quench the thirst of labourers during haymaking.

Heat the water until boiling and dissolve the sugar in it. Pour it on to the gale and add the cream of tartar and juice of the ½ lemon. Cut up the lemon peel and add. Leave to cool, then float the slice of toast on the liquid with the yeast spread upon it. After 24 hours strain and bottle.

This method of wine-making is an old one, for modern recipes no longer use the old 'yeast on toast' method.

Rowan Jelly

crab apples
rowan-berries
sugar

This old preserve is traditionally served with mountain mutton or lamb which might have fed on the fallen berries. A combination of rowan-berries and crab apples gives a more pleasant and less bitter flavour.

Chop up some crab apples, or baking apples if these are not available, and put into a pan with an equal weight of rowan-berries. Cover with water and cook until soft enough to strain through a fine cloth. Do not press through as this makes the jelly cloudy. Measure the juice and return to the pan with 450g (1 pound) of sugar to each 575ml (1 pint). Stir over a low heat until the sugar has melted, then boil for about 10 minutes or until a set is obtained. To test for a set put a small quantity in a saucer in the fridge for a minute or two. Take out and push the surface gently with a finger. If the surface wrinkles, setting point has been reached. Pot while hot.

Blackcurrant Jam

2¾ kg (6 lbs) blackcurrants
2¾ kg (6 lbs) sugar
1¾ litres (3 pints)
   water

Prepare and wash the fruit and put into a pan with the water. Simmer gently until the fruit is tender, then stir and add the sugar. Keep stirring until the sugar is dissolved, then bring to the boil and cook rapidly until the setting point is reached. Pour into hot jars and seal.

makes 5½kg (12 lb)

Rhubarb, Fig and Orange Jam

1¾ kg (4 lbs) rhubarb
100g (4 oz) dried figs
4 lemons
peel from 2 – 4 oranges
1¾ kg (4 lbs) sugar

This and the two chutney recipes are from Penny Glanville, who sells her delicious home-made preserves in Settle market.

Cook and mince the orange and lemon peel, and chop the peeled rhubarb. Put the peels, rhubarb, lemon juice and chopped figs into a large bowl. Add the sugar and stir well. Cover and leave to stand for 24–48 hours. Bring to the boil gently and cook slowly for about 30 minutes, then increase the heat and boil fast until a set is reached.

This jam is difficult to set, it just thickens to an acceptable state.

makes 3½-4½kg (8-10 lb)

Orange Chutney

4 oranges
100g (4 oz) sultanas *or* raisins
2 large apples
1 large onion
225g (½ lb) brown sugar
about 575 ml (1 pint) vinegar
25g (1 oz) salt
6 chopped, dried chillies (no
   seeds)

Peel the oranges, remove any pith and cook the skins. Chop the orange pulp, apples and onion. Mince the peel and put into a pan with the fruit, onions, salt and chillies. Cook gently, adding only as much vinegar as is necessary to prevent sticking. When all the ingredients are cooked, add the sugar and stir well. Continue to cook until the vinegar is absorbed by the chutney and it becomes thick. Put into warmed jars.

Orange, Apple and Rhubarb Chutney

1kg (2 lbs) cooking apples
450g (1 lb) rhubarb
225g (½ lb) sultanas *or* raisins
1 orange

Peel and core the apples. Cook and mince the orange skin, first removing any pith. Peel and chop the rhubarb and cut up the orange pulp. Put all the prepared fruit and sultanas into a pan

450g (1 lb) sugar
575ml (1 pint) vinegar
15g (½ oz) pickling spice

with the vinegar. Add the spice wrapped in a piece of muslin. Cook gently until tender, then stir in the sugar. Cook until thick, remove the pickling spice, and pot into warmed jars.

Pickling Mixture

1kg (2 lbs) salt
50g (2 oz) bay salt (rock salt)
40g (1½ oz) saltpetre
100g (4 oz) Demerara sugar
13⅝ litres (3 gallons) water

This is a pickling mixture which was traditionally used for beef and pork during the preparations for Masham Sheep Fair each September.

Heat some of the water and in it dissolve the salt, bay salt, saltpetre and sugar. Add the rest of the water which may be cold. When the mixture is cold put the meat into it.

Pickled Beetroot

beetroot as desired
2½ litres (4 pints) vinegar
25g (1 oz) salt
50g (2 oz) pickling spice
1 bay leaf
1 blade mace
½ teaspoon ground mixed spice
a pinch of ground nutmeg

Pickled beetroot is a feature of every traditional Yorkshire tea and is also very popular in the north with hot meat and potato pie. The following recipe is used by Isobelle Gott of Lothersdale.

To make the spiced vinegar: put the salt, pickling spice, bay leaf and spices into a pan with the vinegar. Simmer gently for 5 minutes then strain for use. This vinegar can be kept for further use if put into sealed bottles.

Prepare the beetroot carefully, then cook until tender and skin while hot. Cut into thin slices, put into jars, and cover with cold spiced vinegar. Cover securely.

Piccalilli

an assortment of vegetables:
    marrow, cucumber, shallots, onions, cauliflower, green tomatoes—weighing 1¾kg (4 lbs)
salt
1.1 litres (2 pints) white vinegar
25g (1 oz) turmeric
25g (1 oz) flour
25g (1 oz) dry mustard
45g (3 oz) brown sugar
15g (½ oz) ground ginger

Prepare and chop the vegetables; peel and de-seed the marrow, slice the onions and tomatoes, divide the cauliflower into small pieces, cut the cucumber into small chunks. Put into a large bowl and sprinkle all the vegetables with salt. Leave to stand overnight then wash and drain well. Put into a pan with most of the vinegar, retain a little to mix into a smooth paste with the flour and spices. Put this paste into the pan, add the sugar and stir over heat until boiling. Cook for 10 minutes or until thick. Put into clean, warmed jars and seal.

Granny Brown's Piccalilli

any mixture of
  vegetables—about 1¾kg (4 lb):
  cabbage beans onions
  cauliflower radishes
  cucumber carrots green tomatoes
  celery red peppers

pickling vinegar

1 litre (1 quart) vinegar
1 dessertspoon ginger
1 dessertspoon chopped
  chilli peppers
50g (2 oz) shallots
25g (1 oz) garlic
1 dessertspoon salt
2 dessertspoon turmeric
2 dessertspoons flour of
  mustard (dry mustard)

'To a quart of vinegar add ¼ oz of ginger, ¼ oz of long peppers, 2 oz of shallots, 1 oz of garlic and ½ oz of salt, ½ oz of turmeric and ½ oz of flour of mustard. Make this pickling sauce a week before it is needed.

'Prepare the vegetables—cabbage, beans, onions, cauliflowers, radishes, cucumbers, carrots, green tomatoes, celery, red peppers. Pour over with scalding brine and let them lie for two days. Drain thoroughly then wash through with vinegar and drain again. Put into jars and pour over the sauce. The jars must be carefully sealed.'

Yorkshire
Markets

Yorkshire Markets

With the early days of the Industrial Revolution, markets received a new impetus from the constant flow of people into towns. Formerly, rural areas had been served by intinerent pedlars but by the end of the eighteenth century many of these regularly set up stalls in town markets.

Sadly, many markets have now been civilized. The early covered markets have in many places become characterless mirror images of the vast national supermarkets. The buildings remain but the spirit has fled.

Yorkshire people however have had the foresight to defend their old-style markets. The rumbustious cameraderie existing in Doncaster and Halifax is savoured not only by locals but by regular visitors who enjoy coming to shop in the friendly and relaxing atmosphere. Not all markets in large towns are covered. York market is essentially rural in atmosphere; farmers' wives and market gardeners travel from miles around to sell their produce. Yorkshire is still richly endowed with wholesome country-type markets, and the following is a representative selection of some good markets of all sizes, from tiny country street markets to huge covered markets in cities.

Barnsley.   Wednesday, Friday and Saturday. Vast new market hall, ground floor devoted to food. Excellent fish and meat sections with Albert Hirst specialities—black puddings, savoury ducks, Barnsley chops. A good selection of cheeses and of fruit and vegetables. Game in season. Other regional specialities include tripe, cowheel and pig's feet.

Beverley.   The Saturday market. A good selection of meat and cheese always available in this small market with a farm produce stall selling poultry and eggs, occasionally farm butter and game. Home-made cakes sometimes sold.

Bradford.   Daily except Wednesday afternoon. Huge rambling market particularly good for meat of all kinds, fish, game and fruit and vegetables. Very good choice of cheese and a tripe stall selling all kinds of regional delicacies—various tripes (thick seam, honeycomb, black), cowheel, pig's feet, elder, etc.

Bridlington.   Wednesday and Saturday. Tiny street market to be extended shortly. Mainly vegetables and fruit so quality very good. One farm produce stall; eggs, cheese and poultry occasionally.

Dewsbury. Wednesday and Saturday. Interesting market with good choice of fruit and vegetables and a first-class small section for fish.

Doncaster.   Tuesday, Friday and Saturday. An enormous traditional market with both covered and uncovered sections. Market hall selling all kinds of food, very good meat section, also cheeses and home-made bread and cakes. Outside are fruit and vegetables sold by market gardeners. The fish section is splendid, thirty-two stalls. All kinds of game available in season; tripe stalls; curds and farm butter occasionally.

Halifax. Daily except Thursday afternoon. Covered old-style market; very good meat section, mutton and all kinds of cooked meats available—harslet, faggots, elder, tripe, black puddings, etc. Fine selection of cheeses; one stall entirely stocked with free-range eggs; excellent choice of vegetables and fruit, both home-grown and exotic imports.

Harrogate. Daily except Wednesday afternoon. Covered market with small section for meat and fish but quality excellent; tripe, black puddings and game. Three cheese stalls, extensive selection. Fruit and vegetables very good, local produce available. Home-made cakes and locally made butter (Wensleydale). Farm produce stall—poultry, eggs, butter.

Hawes. Tuesday. Small street market with locally grown vegetables, a good selection of fruit and one very good cheese stall. On adjoining main street, shops sell local honey and cheese, curd tarts, parkin and gingerbread.

Hebden Bridge. Thursday. Small open market with emphasis on food. Inexpensive fruit and vegetables; one mobile tripe stall selling produce from own factory—variety of tripe, cowheel, black puddings, elder; small meat stall, good quality; one stall specializing in bacon with typical local delicacies—Yorkshire 'ducks', bacon shanks and dried peas soaking in a large white tub ready to make pea soup or mushy peas.

Huddersfield. Daily except Wednesday. Open market Monday: good choice of fruit and vegetables, one meat stall, one tripe stall. Covered market: good meat section, excellent choice of cheese. All types of fish available in the market arcade, including shark.

Knaresborough. The Wednesday market. Very good for fruit and vegetables, good quality fish and dairy produce. Most English cheese available including Blue Wensleydale. Curds to order from the farm produce stall where home-made butter is sold; home-made biscuits.

Northallerton. Wednesday. Good open market with limited selection of fish but of fine quality. Very good for cheese and fruit and vegetables.

Otley. Friday and Saturday. Small open market, good selection of fruit and vegetables, inexpensive. Small cheese stall with a good choice of cheese including home-made cream cheese and also selling cartons of curds, home-made jams and marmalades. Home-made bread, fruit tarts, crumpets and hot cross buns at Easter.

Ripon. Thursday and Saturday. Large open market with excellent selection of fruit and vegetables, locally grown spinach, rhubarb, leeks, etc. Large fish stall with first class selection available—fresh or dressed crab, rainbow trout, woof, kippers, cockles, mussels, lemon sole, dabs, mackerel, herring, cod, etc.

Scarborough.   Daily except Wednesday afternoon. A covered market with a limited but good quality range of fish, meat and fruit and vegetables. Game is available in season, curds occasionally and a good choice of cheese is offered.

Settle.   Tuesday. Open market is the old square bounded by the Shambles. A good selection of fruit and vegetables, bilberries, Kendal damsons, local produce. Home-cooked meats, savoury and fruit pies; locally made lemon cheese and excellent preserves.

Skipton.   Daily except Thursday. Straggling street market with quite a good choice of fruit and vegetables, cheese and home-made preserves. One good meat stall, limited selection. Shops along main street sell all traditional specialities—parkin, moggy, curd tarts.

Todmorden.   Daily except Tuesday. Covered and open markets with a very good choice of fruit and vegetables, fine choice of meat and cheese; some cooked meats, black puddings, tripe and traditional muffins, oatcakes, etc.

York.   Daily except Monday. Large open market with a separate and excellent fish section with all kinds of fish—woof from Scarborough, skate, crabs, lobsters, kippers, Bridlington cod, cockles, mussels, etc. Very good selection of fruit and vegetables, a large grocery stall and some herbs available in pots. Most interesting section takes place on Saturdays where farmers' wives come to sell free-range eggs, poultry, rabbits, curds, home-made butter, cakes and biscuits including spice cake, parkin, curd tarts and gingerbread; home-made jams and pickles; bunches of leeks or carrots and freshly picked pussy-willow and violets.

Bibliography

Acton, Eliza. *Modern Cookery* (1845).

Beeton, Mrs. *The Book of Household Management* (1859).

Boorde, Andrew. *A Compendyous Regymen or a Dyetary of Healthe* (1562).

Byron, May. *Pot Luck* (Hodder and Stoughton 1914).

Cassell's New Dictionary of Cooking (1912).

Cobbett, William. *Cobbett's Cottage Economy* (1822).

Dodd, George. *The Food of London* (1856).

Easther, A. *A Glossary of the Dialect of Almondbury and Huddersfield* (1883).

Farley, John. *The London Art of Cookery* (1783).

Glasse, Hannah. *The Art of Cookery Made Plain and Easy* (1747).

Hartley, Dorothy. *Food in England* (Macdonald 1954).

Hutchins, Sheila. *English Recipes* (Methuen 1967).

Markham, Gervase. *The English Hus-Wife* (1615).

Martin, Sarah. *The New Experienced English Housekeeper* (1800).

New Improvements on Planting and Gardening (W. Mears 1717).

Nicoll, Lucie G. *The English Cookery Book* (Faber and Faber 1936).

Ozell, Mr. (trans.) *M. Misson's Memoirs: Observations on his Travels over England* (1719).

Peckham, Ann. *The Complete English Cook; or Prudent Housewife* (1767).

Poulson, Joan. *Old Yorkshire Recipes; Old Northern Recipes* (Hendon 1974, 1975).

Raffald, Elizabeth. *The Experienced English Housekeeper* (1796).

Rogers, J. *The Vegetable Cultivator* (1839).

Wilson, Anne. *Food and Drink in Britain* (constable 1973).

The Whole Duty of Woman (1737).

The Yorkshire Federation of Women's Institutes *The Yorkshire Way* (n.d.).

Index